THIS SPECIAL EDITION OF

THE

DEGRADATION OF THE
DEMOCRATIC DOGMA

by Henry Adams

HAS BEEN PRIVATELY PRINTED

FOR THE MEMBERS OF

THE CLASSICS OF LIBERTY LIBRARY

THE CLASSICS OF LIBERTY LIBRARY

THE DEGRADATION OF THE

DEMOCRATIC DOGMA

THE MACMILLAN COMPANY
NEW YORK · BOSTON · CHICAGO · DALLAS
ATLANTA · SAN FRANCISCO

MACMILLAN & CO., Limited
LONDON · BOMBAY · CALCUTTA
MELBOURNE

THE MACMILLAN CO. OF CANADA, Ltd.
TORONTO

THE

DEGRADATION OF THE DEMOCRATIC DOGMA

BY

HENRY ADAMS

WITH AN INTRODUCTION BY

BROOKS ADAMS

New York

THE MACMILLAN COMPANY

1920

Norwood Press
J. S. Cushing Co. — Berwick & Smith Co.
Norwood, Mass., U.S.A.

INTRODUCTORY NOTE

BEFORE submitting the following pages to the public, I have a few words to say, lest my purpose should be misunderstood. I want to make it clear, once for all, that I am not proposing to write anything approaching to a memoir of my brother. He has written his memoirs for himself. For me to try to improve on them would be superfluous, not to say impertinent. Nor do I suggest any criticism of his essays which are annexed. These I have long thought unanswerable. With their conclusions I fully agree. I have no further comment to make.

I am attempting something quite different from this. I am seeking to tell the story of a movement in thought which has, for the last century, been developing in my family, and which closes with the "Essay on Phase," which ends this volume.

At this particular juncture of human affairs the tendency is very strong throughout the world to deify the democratic dogma, and to look to democracy to accomplish pretty promptly some approach to a millennium among men.

This form of belief was strong in my family a century ago, and found expression through my grandfather, John Quincy Adams, who made the realization thereof the work and ambition of his life and who, when he grew old, practically gave his life for the cause. As an apostle of this doctrine, I take it, he must always be one of the most commanding figures in our history, when he comes to be fully understood, and as such I give him the chief place in my story. He based his hopes of success, in his supreme effort, on the belief that God, in whose existence, at that period in his life, he did not doubt, favored him, and would aid him; but he died declaring that God had abandoned him, and was only kept from confessing agnosticism by his love and veneration for his mother, which even passed the adoration of Catholics for the Virgin, and whose memory was an obstacle which he could not surmount, when it came to renouncing his dream of immortality. But so far as he had watched, during a lifetime, the progress of the democrat toward perfection, he had little to say in the way of hope. And so he died. His life was a tragedy, ending in the Civil War, which he had long foreseen approaching, but which he had been unable to do anything to avert. Yet the greatest tragedy of all for us, and for all optimists who believe in the advent of perfection through the influence of democracy, is the condition in which we have been left since the close of the war. I wish to point out that the Civil War was fought, presumably, to enforce the democratic principle "of the natural equality of man, and the possession of certain rights of which he cannot be deprived by violence." But, viewed in this light, our country is as much in the midst of a social war now as she was when Lincoln died. And she is so because she has tried to ignore certain fundamental facts which are stronger than democratic theories. I suppose that the time has now come when I must refer to myself as a part of this family tree, although no work of mine has any interest for the present discussion save in so far as something I may have said or written may have been suggestive to Henry. Like Henry, I inherited a belief in the great democratic dogma, as I inherited my pew in the church at Quincy, but, as I have explained in my preface, in my early middle life I fell into difficulties which only good fortune prevented from turning out as tragically for me, as did the election of 1828 for my ancestor. In this crisis of my fate I learned, as a lawyer and a student of history and of economics, to look on man, in the light of the evidence of unnumbered centuries, as a pure automaton, who is moved along the paths of least resistance by forces over which he has no control. In short, I reverted to the pure

Calvinistic philosophy. As I perceived that the strongest of human passions are fear and greed, I inferred that so much and no more might be expected from a pure democracy as might be expected from any automaton so actuated. As a forecast I suggested that the first great social movement we might expect, should be the advent of something resembling a usurer's paradise, to be presently followed by some such convulsion as has always formed a part of such conditions since the beginning of time. The precedents are plenty. Lastly, I come to Henry's philosophy, which I conceive stands by the side of his grandfather's philosophy, as the most interesting discussion of the great democratic dogma of modern times. Henry has followed very much his grandfather's scientific methods, saving so far as those methods turned upon religion, and, I apprehend, that Henry has demonstrated certain facts. The first great fact is that science is sunk in such chaos that, from the teachings of science, it is impossible to show that the world itself, or man as a portion of the world, has been evolved in obedience to any single power which might be called a unified creator. Its tendency is always to suggest complexity as a motor. Therefore democracy must partake of the complexity of its infinitely complex creator, and ultimately end in chaos. Meanwhile society is steadily undergoing a degradation of vital energy. I will not enter further now upon the arguments set forth in the "Letter to Teachers" and in "Phase." They speak for themselves.

Nevertheless, I submit that these collective results, being those drawn by one family from their experience and study throughout an entire century, and which have been reached under an environment the most favorable possible toward creating a belief in the great democratic dogma, had it been in any degree true, are at least worthy of the calm consideration of fair-minded persons.

When my grandfather, John Quincy Adams, was preparing his report on "Weights and Measures," which has since his death become so famous in the scientific world, he bitterly complained that, at Washington, he could find no kindred mind to whom he could confide his perplexities and from whom he could draw a stimulant. In the same way, when I came to editing the philosophical essays of my brother, I acutely felt the lack of a kindly scientist, to whom I could go to guard me against my own imcompetence and blunders. At length Mr. Ford suggested that I should apply to Professor Bumstead of Yale, to whom he intimated that he thought my brother had submitted his manuscript years ago, before his illness. I greedily seized upon the hint, and Professor Bumstead not only read the papers I sent him with the utmost kindness, but actually took the trouble to visit me at Quincy, and talk my problems over with me after dinner, in my own house. I need not say that the professor entirely relieved my mind, and that from the day of his visit I have had no fear that Henry's meaning shall be deformed by my negligence or ignorance. His papers, as they are presented, are the accurate expression of his thought. As an editor my responsibility ends there. And this brings me to my obligation to my old friend Mr. Worthington Ford of the Massachusetts Historical Society. As the public perhaps knows to its cost, I have, during the past quarter of a century, now and then published books, and in my typographical and other difficulties, I have not hesitated to victimize Mr. Ford ruthlessly, to my incapacity or convenience. And Mr. Ford has endured the infliction, like a good fellow and a good friend to Henry and me. In the present emergency I applied to Mr. Ford at once, and with absolute success. Without his knowledge of my brother's library, I could not have presented the last corrections Henry made in the papers which I now submit, nor should I have known enough to apply to Professor Bumstead without whom I should hardly have dared to venture on my task. But Mr. Ford's kindness did not stop here, by any means. He it was who knew about, and secured, the last annotations which my brother made to his "Letter to Teachers," and he it was who has read the proof, and has taken care that all Henry's citations of authorities, in various languages, are correct in the text. More than this: he offered to prepare, and has prepared, the index for me. I need not say how much better his work is than mine would have been, for making an index is an art, which displays the book, and Mr. Ford, as all know who know anything, is the leading authority on such work, in America if not in the world, as I incline very strongly to think. Therefore, I have consented to accept his kind and generous offers, although by so doing I have shirked my own share of my task. The public, however, gains.

And so I come to my last and, it may be, my chiefest obligation. When it was proposed that I should publish my brother's philosophical remains, with an introduction, I lightly assented, not appreciating the gravity of the work before me, nor the paucity of time in which to do it. For the publishers insisted that I should be ready before the year closed, else the book would lose its interest. So I began in April, but I soon realized my error. I was not writing, in any sense, a biography; but no author, especially no philosopher, can be understood, unless his works be laid before the public with such a sketch of his environment and his inheritance as shall make intelligible

the forces social, economic and family, which produced
him. Least of all could this be done with so complex a
creature as was my brother Henry.

And, as I worked, my task grew upon me until I perceived that I could never hope to put Henry in his true
place in modern intellectual development, unless I went
back to the foundation of the Republic, if not to the
Reformation. But to do so would require a bulky volume
unfit to prefix to such seemingly slender essays as these;
besides being foreign to what the publishers wanted.

Thus hampered, I sought to compress; and I made sad
work of it, the more so as I neared my limit of time. In
June the end came, and I despaired. I realized that I
could not print what I had produced; it was disjointed
and incohesive beyond tolerance. In this dilemma I
turned to my old friend Mrs. Jones of New York, who,
besides having for many years advised some of the chief
publishing houses of New York as to the relative worth of
proposed manuscripts, and thereby having acquired a
vast experience in what the public demands, had been
for half a lifetime intimate with both Henry and me.

Much perplexed, I laid my manuscript before her, saying, "This fragment is bad; I cannot publish it as it
stands, but I know not how to better it." What should
I do? In the kindest way in the world she read my

failure over more than once, and then she said to me, "Your 'Introduction' is bad, I agree, but it may not be irreclaimable." And she made me some suggestions. These I followed as well as time permitted, and now I have it much on my mind to tell any possible future readers of this book that, if they shall find, at the end of their perusal of the volume, they retain in their minds any clear conception of the figures I introduce, or of the work they tried to do, or of the part they sought to play, in the society in which they lived, they will owe their concept far more to her than to me. My grandfather in especial will, if I shall succeed, live, as it were again, but in a new light, because of her sympathy with and comprehension of his most fervent ambitions, his efforts and his disasters, ending in his death, — a martyr to his belief in God, education, and science.

BROOKS ADAMS.

QUINCY,
2d September, 1919.

CONTENTS

	PAGE
INTRODUCTORY NOTE	V
THE HERITAGE OF HENRY ADAMS	1
THE TENDENCY OF HISTORY	125
A LETTER TO AMERICAN TEACHERS OF HISTORY . .	137
The Problem	140
The Solutions	209
THE RULE OF PHASE APPLIED TO HISTORY . . .	267

THE DEGRADATION OF THE DEMOCRATIC DOGMA

THE HERITAGE OF HENRY ADAMS

TAKEN for all in all, my brother Henry was distinctly the most cultivated and stimulating man, of my own generation, whom I ever knew intimately. I owe more to his than to any other mind, including that of my father, and I can say no more. Yet none of us is quite perfect, and I must frankly admit that Henry had certain intellectual peculiarities without allowing for which I deem it impossible to fully appreciate either the work he did or his way of doing it.

And, to begin with, Henry was never, I fear, quite frank with himself or with others ; certainly he was not with me, and yet I fancy that I was, in some respects, perhaps his most intimate friend. I know well that he was mine ; that I valued his opinion more than that of any one on earth, if I could only get it, and that I would go far to obtain it. Still, even with me, Henry was always shy and oversensitive and disliked disagreeable subjects.

Hence he would surround himself with different defences, all of them calculated to repel tactless advances, and on these defences few of us cared to intrude. Personally I at least, always avoided them.

One of these was that, when his wife died, in 1884, he insisted that he also died to the world. In plain English, business bored him, and he threw all such details on us vulgarians who were, in his judgment, fit for no better. Probably he was right. Also he dearly loved paradox, and nothing amused him more than propounding something which he knew would startle his guests or rouse in them the spirit of contradiction. Some of these paradoxes he has related in his "Education." Perhaps his favorite, and the one he was always venting on me to see how I would take it, was the proposition that the man, especially the soldier, is a coarse brute, and the woman intellectually his superior ; whence he deduced his peculiar cult of the Virgin, as an ideal of intellect and not of sex, which I admit, to me, rather deforms *Mont Saint Michel and Chartres*, when carried to the extreme to which he sometimes carried it. And yet, on the other hand, I appreciated the problem he had in mind, and which he wished to discuss, — the dissolution of the modern family. On that head he was serious, and, so I suppose, are we all. And the more we reflect on this subject, the more overshadowing it grows and the more alarming, not to say terrifying, it becomes. At all events to me.

For my part, I have for the last twenty years at least, contemplated the domestic relations, as a lawyer, with consternation. Henry, on the whole, was always inclined to be impatient with my legal theories, but in this matter he would listen to me. "You are by way of being an archæologist," I would say to him, " and I want to know whether in all your reading you have ever encountered the man who could explain the origin of the family, and how it came to cohere? I assume that long before the ice cap shrank from off this northern continent civilization, such as it was, rested on the family, and that it always had so rested. All our legal notions, which are of consequence, are derived thence. Of that I am sure. Such conceptions, for example, as the right to hold private property, the law of inheritance, the title to property itself, and more than this the right to personal safety as developed in the criminal law. Moreover the family system is the creation of the woman rather than that of the man. The man has wandered. He has been the soldier, the sailor, the hunter, the fisher, the trader, and the herdsman. All of these are occupations more or less dangerous, and which exact absences from home. The woman, on the contrary, has lived at home and has cared for the children. Thus she has acted as the social cement, and she has sustained the arch on which the social fabric has rested. And now, behold, the woman has renounced her job, she is ashamed of her sex, and I know not how man can replace her. One sex alone cannot vivify a civilization. What do you say?"

Henry could answer the question no more than I, but he loved to play with it. I never said, by the way, or even intimated that the American woman is more of a failure than another. My thesis was that all women, under modern conditions, ceased automatically to be cohesive. Henry sought to amplify the problem.

He has told us in his memoirs, with what gusto he would ask some woman sitting near him, at his own table, why the American woman was a failure. He knew perfectly well what he wished to imply and the response he sought to elicit, but to have explained himself would have spoiled his fun. If he had said that, in these latter days, the woman has become volatilized so excessively that she wanders more freely and constantly than does the man, and therefore rather acts as a dissolvent than as a cement, he might have been forced into a lecture on jurisprudence, which would have been intolerable. Therefore he sat quiet, grinned, and listened to what the women said. Nor was I ever myself quite sure how much he believed in his own paradoxes. He certainly believed that the family tie was weakening and that the woman was volatilizing; but touching her intellectual superiority it was another matter. He did believe in the superior energy of the maternal instinct, but the inference presumably was that, with the American woman in especial, precisely in proportion as she increased her independence, she diminished her weight and her importance in the social scale. She separated into a finite atom, and ceased to be the heart of the social unit.

Most of us would readily have admitted so much, but to have stopped there would have spoiled sport, so he insisted on being taken quite seriously. He always reminded me of the story we boys used to have in college about Professor Benjamin Peirce, who was sometimes obscure to us youngsters. One day when lecturing at the blackboard he casually observed that an equation, which he wrote down, "obviously" was the equivalent of another, which he proceeded also to write down before us. An undergraduate, rather bolder than the rest, or possibly more intelligent, having watched with bewilderment, ventured to interrupt with, "I beg pardon, professor, but I don't think I quite follow." "Don't you?" said Benny, kindly but rather scornfully. "Can you then follow this?" Whereupon he filled two boards with formulæ. And so it was with Henry. I used to sit and listen with amusement almost equal to his own. But I think in his "Education" he has carried his joke, at times, perhaps a little too far for his own fame.

For instance, he poses, more or less throughout his book, as having been a failure and a disappointed man. He was neither the one nor the other, as he knew well. He was not a failure, for he succeeded, and succeeded brilliantly, in whatever he undertook, where success was possible; and he was not disappointed, for the world gave him everything he would take. He would not have touched office in any form, had it been offered. He valued his liberty and his perfect independence too much to part with it at, what he would have thought, so vile a price. What he really cared for, as he has intimated in his "Education," was social consideration, and this he had wherever he chose to live. No man could have been more petted than he at Cambridge. I know, for I lived with him. But he soon tired of Cambridge because Cambridge did not socially amuse him. So pretty soon after his marriage, he and his wife moved to Washington, where they lived contentedly until her death; when he began wandering again. Finally he cast anchor in Paris, which suited him best of all, I think, as he aged; and it was in these latter years that I was most intimate with him. It was in these later years, also, that he became absorbed in his philosophy wherein he was intensely serious, and it is largely because I think that he has hardly done justice to this side of his character that I have written this preface, to serve as a sort of counterpoise, as it were, to his "Education," where he has loved to dilate on what he thought more amusing.

Indeed, to speak the truth, I rather tried to avoid his lighter social circle, a disposition which I think he noticed and allowed for. And I have even conjectured that, because of this tendency of mine, he chose a moment when he was in Washington and I in Quincy to send me the following essay on "Phase," for my opinion, instead of keeping it for one of my visits to his house, and talking it over with me there. At all events it happened that, soon after I had read it and warmly approved it and urged him to publish it, he was stricken with the illness which incapacitated him for work, and thenceforward I heard no more of "Phase." I took it for granted that he felt unequal to putting "Phase" through the press, even were he satisfied with the form in which it stood, which I doubted, for Henry stickled for form. Therefore in bringing it out as he left it eight years ago, I am acting as his trustee, and I have definite ideas of what my duty is toward such a trust.

In the first place I should try to show him, as nearly

as may be, as he appeared to me in those days when we
discussed these questions; though, unhappily, I can give
to those who never knew him no conception of his sug-
gestiveness nor of his power. But above all I should
seek to make others feel, as he always made me feel,
that he never trifled with what were to both of us serious
subjects, dealing as they mostly did, either with the lives
of our predecessors or with our own future. A very
large part of this time I was busy with sundry books of
my own which have since appeared, but during another
portion I was occupied with a memoir of John Quincy
Adams which I then expected to publish and whose
chapters I sent to Henry for his revision, as I finished
them. In reply Henry returned me notes and letters
which would almost fill a volume by themselves, and
which gave me abundant food for meditation. The
upshot of it all was that I decided to suppress the book
in spite of Henry's remonstrances.

And now as I look back through the vista of a dozen
years and in the light of these two essays, I am more
certain than ever that I was right. I am clear that
neither Henry nor I, when I was writing those chapters,
had as yet come to the point at which we could altogether appreciate our ancestor. John Quincy Adams
was not only a complex man, who stood at least a genera-

tion ahead of his time, but he was a scientist of the first force. The same problems vexed him as he grew old, which have vexed Henry and me now for all our later lives, and it may well be that my attempt to write my grandfather's story may have stimulated Henry to compose these essays. But whether it did or did not, the same train of thought and manner of thinking is obvious enough in the older and in the younger generation, and what is most remarkable is the persistence of the same caste of intelligence in the grandfather and grandson, the scientific mixed with the political, which made the older man reject with horror a scientific theory forced upon him by circumstances, which the younger man has accepted, if not with approbation, at least with resignation, and at so relatively short an interval of time.

On February 18, 1909, Henry wrote me a very long letter, from which I extract the following paragraph, only because it expresses the view which I wish to accentuate, and because it bears quite as strongly on Henry's then attitude of mind and his subsequent development, as it does on that of J. Q. Adams.

"No one with the intelligence of an average monkey will try to tell a story without leading up to its point. Your tragedy will be indicated as it is in the lives of us all, by the chief failure, which is, in your case, the Presidency.

To me, the old gentleman's Presidency appears always as lurid, — which is not the impression made on me by his father's defeat, — and I see the age of Andrew Jackson and the cotton planters much as I see the age of the Valois or Honorius, — that is, with profound horror."

And touching the episode of the Presidency, Henry was, in my opinion, perfectly right. The Presidency was the tragedy of our grandfather's life because it injected into his mind the first doubt as to whether there were a God, and whether this life had a purpose.

That from the moment of his defeat, in 1828, his life took the form of a tragedy was through no fault of his, but because, by the nature of human affairs, he was forced, by bitter experience, to admit that science and education offer no solution to our difficulties, but possibly on the contrary aggravate them. In short, John Quincy Adams, at the opening of his Presidency, fell into the vortex of the movement which is now, apparently, only culminating, and of which the Reformation itself was the prelude. He himself, with the knowledge at hand, could not see the relation of cause and effect as we can. But he was conscious of the movement, and the unconscious thought stimulated thereby, which harassed him, may still be read in his prayers to God for defence against his own mind, as he neared the end.

So far as Henry himself is concerned I take it that in 1909 when he was writing to me on his grandfather, he still took the conventional view of the man, if I may call it so. That is to say, he considered that John Quincy Adams had been a political man, actuated by ordinary political feelings; whereas I believe him to have been an idealistic philosopher who sought with absolute disinterestedness to put the Union upon a plane of civilization which would have averted the Civil and might have altered the complexion of the recent War; who failed, as all men must fail who harbor such a purpose, and who almost with his last breath resigned himself and his ambitions to fate. To me the picture of the old man in his last days, submitting to the destiny which he could not avert but which he had long seen approaching, is pathetic, and is not unlike that of his grandson who has written for our contemplation his regret at the loss of religious faith, and his resignation to resistless nature, in "Phase." The following extract, therefore, seems to me hardly fair. Doubtless Henry would modify it were it to be rewritten now. Nevertheless it is to me highly suggestive and therefore worth quoting.

"Yet, setting my own wicked nature aside, this familiar picture of the old man in the prize ring, much as I love it, interests me less than the documents you quote to show the steps of degradation that forced him into it against his will. Especially the letter to Upham of February 2, 1837, which is quite new to me, has given me cause for much thought. As I read, between its lines, the bitterness of his failure, and the intensity of his regret at having served the Sable Genius of the South, are immensely tragic — so much so that he shrank from realizing its whole meaning even to himself. From the year 1828, life took to him the character of tragedy. With the same old self-mortification which he and we have all, more or less, inherited from Calvinism, I believe, if he had read what I have written to you about his early life, he would have beaten his breast, and cried his culp, and begged the forgiveness of his God, although I can't make much of his God anyway."

I radically dissent from all this now as I did then.

CHAPTER I

The Heritage of Henry Adams

I AM trying, throughout this Introduction, to present the minds of these two powerful and original men, the grandfather and the grandson, in their true relation, as they stood, often unconsciously, first toward each other, and secondly toward that movement of democratic society, during the past century, which imposed on them the task of attempting to fathom the science and meaning of history. Plainly my function would be impossible were I not to expose in the first place, something of the constraining antecedents of both.

John Quincy Adams appears to me to be the most interesting and suggestive personage of the early nineteenth century, as my brother Henry is, in his philosophy, certainly one of the most so of the present century; but it is impossible to understand the elder, as it is the younger, man unless we begin by appreciating the education and the circumstances which made them what they were. George Washington was the model and the master of Adams, and George Washington had a constructive theory, which John Quincy Adams imbibed and strove to carry into effect, by which he hoped to consolidate a vast American community from which slavery should be eliminated and which should act as a universal pacifier. And Washington's topographical theory, on which all else rested, was shortly this:

In his wanderings in early life in the western wilderness, Washington conceived the principle that a consolidated community which should have the energy to cohere must be the product of a social system resting on converging highways, and, in the case before him, those highways must evidently be the Potomac and Ohio rivers connected by a canal. The point at which this main trunk avenue from west to east met the ocean must, from the nature of things, be somewhere near the site he afterward chose for the national capital, where a great industrial development might easily be stimulated; and with an energetic industrial development of their iron and coal, Maryland and Virginia must automatically become free. Accordingly as early as 1770 he wrote to Governor Johnson of Maryland as follows:

"There is the strongest speculative proof in the world to me of the immense advantages which Virginia and Maryland might derive (and at a very small comparative expense) by making the Potomac channel of commerce between Great Britain, and that immense Territory . . . [the Mississippi Valley] the advantages of which are too great, and too obvious, I should think, to become the subject of serious debate, but which, through ill-timed parsimony and supineness, may be wrested from us and conducted through other channels, . . . How difficult it will be to divert it afterward, time only can show."[1]

Pushing his plan steadily, Washington in 1775 thought himself near success, but when the Revolutionary War broke out he had to leave Mount Vernon and take command of the army. Eight years of fighting only confirmed his faith in his plan, and after the peace he had reached the unalterable conviction that unless the west could be bound to the east by practicable trade routes American civilization must sink in chaos. At that particular moment the most threatening line of cleavage lay along the Alleghany Mountains, but no intelligent man could doubt that the cohesion between the North and South was almost equally precarious.

With his usual good sense Washington turned to the most pressing danger first and also to the one most easily to be averted. The chief danger of division which Washington foresaw was that the western country would

[1] Washington to Johnson, Congressional Documents, 1st Session, 19th Congress, Report No. 228, p. 28.

be repelled by the difficulty of the mountain trails, but would be correspondingly attracted toward the Gulf by the grade of the water shed. Louisiana then was, of course, in foreign hands. Conversely the chief threat Washington perceived for the success of his scheme was competition by the route of Lake Erie and the Hudson, but he expected to enjoy at least a temporary advantage by the British occupation of Niagara, and the other strategic points on the Lakes, which would give his canal, for the time, a monopoly ; and once fixed in a given route travel would be measurably stable.

Having reached these conclusions he obtained a charter for his canal from the Virginia legislature in 1785, and thereafter the stockholders elected him as their president. He knew well enough that his first difficulty would be with conflicting jurisdictions and this led him to write to a number of gentlemen to meet at Mount Vernon, whence came by successive gradations the gathering at Annapolis and the convention at Philadelphia, which framed the Constitution of the United States. The adoption of the Constitution incidentally ruined the Potomac Canal, since Washington was, as President of the Union, interdicted from private speculations, and there was no one to replace him as a canal president in Virginia, while his patriotism caused him to open the northern route, by obtaining the cession of the posts, held by Great Britain, through Jay's treaty.

Washington's conception of a national capital corresponded in magnificence with his plan for the concentration of the nation. Built on converging avenues, it was to be adapted at once to military, commercial, administrative, and educational purposes, for at its heart was to be organized the university which was to serve as the brain of the corporeal system developed by the highways. The university was, in fine, to fix a standard of collective thought. In Washington's judgment the university could and should be made to be at once the most delicate, the most pervasive, and the most effective instrument for the amalgamation of a united people, and he strongly urged it upon Congress. As he himself said, his mind had been unable to contemplate any plan more likely "to spread systematic ideas through all parts of the rising empire" than would such an university. And as Washington believed in centralized education as essential to any true national life, so doubtless he would have advocated collective highway construction had he not himself been directly interested in what was to be, according to him, the main artery of commerce. Nor did Washington's views stop here. A necessary adjunct to the system of development which

c

he projected was the rooting out of slavery, for, according to him, nothing else could perpetuate the Union, and slavery, as Washington admitted to himself, could only [1] be peacefully abolished when it ceased to pay, since "the motives which predominate most in human affairs are self-love and self-interest." But slavery could only cease to pay when Virginia became industrial, and this was probably one of the main reasons why Washington advocated domestic industry. Much relating to this subject occurs in his correspondence. After he became President he grew more reticent, but he went to the verge of what he thought proper in urging Governor Randolph to induce certain Englishmen to set up woollen mills within the state. In short, at this stage of American social development, or at the time when Adams first began to take an intelligent interest in public problems, most intelligent Virginians deplored slavery. George Mason thought it a curse, degrading the population and condemning the community to agriculture and relative poverty, while Jefferson and Wyeth were in substance abolitionists, and Washington, as an eminent man of business, disliked and opposed servile labor because of its wastefulness. The difficulty in those days lay not here, but further south in South Carolina and Georgia,

[1] Retrospections of America, John Bernard, edition of 1887, p. 91.

who would enter into no compact with the North which did not guarantee them their property. Rutledge of South Carolina stated with exactness the true southern position, as it was afterward held universally south of the Potomac: "Religion and humanity have nothing to do with this question. Interest alone is the governing principle with nations. The true question is whether the Southern States shall or shall not be parties to the Union."

Finally a bargain was struck. The North agreed that, in computing the population entitled to representation in the House of Representatives and in the Electoral College, slaves should be counted in the ratio of three fifths of their number, that fugitive slaves should be surrendered to their owners wherever found, and that the United States should protect the states against domestic violence.

Verily, momentous issues hinged upon the success of Washington's experiment, for had Virginia developed industrially she must have become free, and with Virginia free there could have been no Civil War. But in 1799 Washington died, leaving his scheme of converging highways embryonic, and his federal capital, which should have been the focus of American exchanges, industry, and thought, little better than a wilderness. And he failed because he could not bring it about that his canal should, at that precise moment of time, be built by government funds or, in other words, collectively. Also by 1804 his failure and the cause thereof had become apparent. And it was then that John Quincy Adams took up the theory of constructive centralization, not indeed precisely at the point at which Washington had left it, but with the expansion due to the operation upon the problem of a profound scientific mind. Adams could not so early understand that science might defeat its own intended end.

Before entering the Senate in 1803 Adams had probably never reflected upon the relation of transportation to civilization, but he could not have dwelt long at what Washington proposed to have made the focus of western vitality without observing the absence of energy at the heart. Thus he soon reached the same conclusion which Washington had reached long before, that a highly organized community could only be the offspring of a sound system of highways and that effective highways should be built by the State since, were highways built as a speculation by private persons, the common welfare must be subordinated to private profit. Thus he evolved his theory of internal improvements, which moulded his whole later life.

Mr. Adams said in conversation with another member

of Congress, T. R. Mitchell, in 1831 : "I was no worshipper of the tariff, but of internal improvement, for the pursuit of which by Congress, as a system, I claimed to be the first mover.   It was by a resolution which I offered to the Senate of the United States on the 23d of February, 1807." [1]

Adams' resolution under another name brought forth Gallatin's well-known report, which Clay afterward advocated, but which Adams alone succeeded in formulating in his message to Congress in 1825, which embodied this doctrine, and which was set aside by Jackson, but which must be read by any one who would understand this phase of American development.

Most unfortunately for all concerned Adams' connection with internal improvements at this stage of the movement was short.   A few days after he offered his resolution, the session closed.   The next June the *Leopard* fired upon the *Chesapeake;* in consequence Adams voted for the embargo, whereupon he resigned from the Senate, and in 1809 was sent to Russia by Mr. Madison.

[1] Diary VIII, 444.

Resolved, "That the Secretary of the Treasury be directed to prepare and report to the Senate, at their next session, a plan for the application of such means as are constitutionally within the power of Congress, to the purposes of opening roads, for removing obstructions in rivers, and making canals; together with a statement of the undertakings of that nature now existing within the United States which, as objects of public improvement, may require and deserve the aid of government."

It is well to observe that at this period the African slave trade was suppressed, which raised the price of slaves and thus tended to throw slave breeding upon the border states, such as Virginia, making it gradually her most profitable industry. Adams only returned in 1817 to take charge of the State Department, and at once plunged into the Florida controversy, which involved the defence of Jackson for the execution of Arbuthnot and Ambrister, and absolutely absorbed his attention until the rise of the Missouri question in 1819. Meanwhile, however, the whole economic equilibrium of the country had been shifted by the appearance of the cotton gin. In 1792 Eli Whitney, a native of Massachusetts and a graduate of Yale, invented the cotton gin, whose purpose was to separate the cotton seed from the fibre, which it had been theretofore extremely tedious and expensive to do by hand. The machine was a success and though Whitney was robbed of his invention, he revolutionized cotton planting by making it highly lucrative, so much so that in 1830 the crop reached one million bales. The breeding of slaves for the cultivation of this cotton thus became more profitable in Virginia than industry in iron and coal. Finally Virginia came to export forty thousand blacks annually for the purpose, and it was then that Mr. Adams came, by the pressure of events, to consider the Missouri question which arose therefrom. His diary is full of references to it. In his view the whole complexion of western civilization turned upon its right determination. Peace and war even were directly involved, and from the outset, as early as January, 1820, it had fixed his attention and in an aspect quite diverse from that which had presented itself to Washington:

"The Missouri question has taken such hold of my feelings and imagination that, finding my ideas connected with it very numerous, but confused for want of arrangement, I have within these few days begun to commit them to paper loosely as they arise in my mind. There are views of the subject which have not yet been taken by any of the speakers or writers by whom they have been discussed — views which the time has not yet arrived for presenting to the public, but which in all probability it will be necessary to present hereafter. I take it for granted that the present question is a mere preamble — a title-page to a great tragic volume. I have reserved my opinions upon it, as it has been obviously proper for me to do. The time may, and I think will, come when it will be my duty equally clear to give my opinion, and it is even now proper for me to begin the preparation of myself for that emergency. The

President thinks this question will be winked away by a compromise. But so do not I. Much am I mistaken if it is not destined to survive his political and individual life and mine." [1]

Thus the problem was gradually assuming in the mind of Adams both a scientific and a religious aspect, and I think that I cannot do better than to insert here the letter to Mr. Upham to which Henry alluded as explaining the scientific side of his program. Mr. Upham was a Salem clergyman who had asked Mr. Adams for details wherewith to write a notice of his life.

According to Adams' own repeated and most solemn asseverations made to himself as he came to die, his highest aspiration, his dearest hope, almost from his youth up, had been by his sustained support of applied science to rank as one of the benefactors of mankind. He admitted that he had failed.

WASHINGTON, 2 Feb., 1837.

REV. CHARLES W. UPHAM,
        Salem, Mass.

MY DEAR SIR:

I fear I have done and can do little good in the world. And my life will end in disappointment of the good which I would have done, had I been permitted. The great effort of my administration was to mature into a permanent and regular system the application of all the

[1] Diary IV, 502, January 10, 1820.

superfluous revenue of the Union to internal improvement which at this day would have afforded high wages and constant employment to hundreds of thousands of laborers, and in which every dollar expended would have repaid itself fourfold in the enhanced value of the public lands.   With this system in ten years from this day the surface of the whole Union would have been checkered over with railroads and canals.   It may still be done half a century later and with the limping gait of State legislature and private adventure.   I would have done it in the administration of the affairs of the nation.   I laid the foundation of it all by a resolution offered to the Senate of the United States in 1806, and adopted under another's name (the Journals of the Senate are my vouchers.)[1]

When I came to the presidency the principle of internal improvement was swelling the tide of public prosperity, till the Sable Genius of the South saw the signs of his own inevitable downfall in the unparalleled progress of the general welfare of the North, and fell to cursing the tariff, and internal improvement, and raised the standard of free trade, nullification, and state rights.   I fell and with me fell, I fear never to rise again, certainly never to rise again in my day, the system of internal improvement by means of national energies.   The great object of my life therefore, as applied to the administration of the government of the United States, has failed.   The American Union, as a moral person in the family of nations, is to live from hand to mouth, and to cast away instead of using for the improvement of its own condition, the bounties of Providence.

But, after all, was there a Providence?

[1] It was in fact presented on February 23, 1807, Diary VIII, 444.

This must serve as my exposition of Mr. Adams' policy of collective administration as a statesman and as a Christian, which he had evolved on the theory that man is a reasoning animal and that there is a God or a conscious ruler of the universe, whom man can intelligently serve and with whom he can covenant. Assuming that there was in existence such a universe and such a benevolent God, Mr. Adams went on to explain as a scientific fact that a volume of energy lay stored within the Union, which as an administrator he could have developed had he been able to work at leisure and had he been supported by his Creator. Also this potential energy would have raised the people of this country beyond the danger of severe economic competition, practically, forever. Such a consummation had, however, been made impossible by the growth of the planting, or slave interest, permitted by the Almighty, which was an offence to God. This was a catastrophe which he could never understand nor forget — supposing there to have been a Providence. The substance of this appears in the following extract from a very famous address made by him in 1842, almost at the close of his active political life, and when he appreciated that Civil War was imminent.

"The Southern or Slave party, outnumbered by the

free, are cemented together by a common, intense interest of property to the amount of $1,200,000,000 in human beings, the very existence of which is neither allowed nor tolerated in the North. . . . The total abandonment by President Jackson, of all internal improvement by the authority of Congress, and of all national protection to domestic industry, was a part of the same system, which, in the message of December, 1832, openly recommended to give away gratuitously all the public lands, and renounce forever all idea of raising any revenue from them. This was nullification in its most odious feature. The public lands are the richest inheritance ever bestowed by a bountiful Creator upon any national community. All the mines of gold and silver and precious stones on the face or in the bowels of the globe, are in value compared to them, but the dust of the balance. Ages upon ages of continual progressive improvement, physical, moral, political, in the condition of the whole people of this Union, were stored up in the possession and disposal of these lands. . . .

"I had long entertained and cherished the hope that these public lands were among the chosen instruments of Almighty power, . . . of improving the condition of man, by establishing the practical, self-evident truth of the natural equality and brotherhood of all mankind, as the foundation of all human government, and by banishing slavery and war from the earth. . . . The project first proclaimed by Andrew Jackson, . . . of giving away the national inheritance to private land jobbers, or to the states in which they lie . . . was the consummation of the Maysville road veto policy . . . to perpetuate the institution of slavery and its dominion over the North American Union. [1]

"I have earnestly hoped that those states themselves would at no distant day abolish slavery. My hopes of these events are not wholly abandoned but weakened and deferred. The interdiction of the African slave trade has had the unfortunate effect of giving the monopoly of the slave-breeding trade to Maryland and Virginia, and it is lamentable to see that the most sordid of passions has thus been enlisted on the side of perpetual slavery."

Having now explained in his own words Mr. Adams' opinions as a statesman and as a scientist touching national collective administrative development, we approach what to him was the most vital of all questions, and that was the relation of his policy of internal improvement to God. First of all I must premise that, as a Christian, Mr. Adams still at this date, in theory, believed, and probably at the time of his election to the presidency

[1] Address to Constituents, Sept. 17, 1842, pp. 22, 23, 24, 51, 52.

believed without a doubt, in the existence of a Supreme and omnipotent Creator of the world, whose nature was benign, and of a "crucified Saviour" who proclaimed immortal life and who preached peace on earth, good-will to men, the natural equality of all mankind, and the law, "Thou shalt love thy neighbor as thyself." Such being in general his theological belief,[1] he thus stated his conception of the relation which this divine principle bore to his duty to develop by all means in his power the resources of the United States in such a manner as should conduce most to the moral elevation and physical well-being of the whole people. Such a movement in his view, as I have already shown, hinged on the scientific development of internal resources, so that they might be utilized without waste.

QUINCY, 13 July, 1837.

REV. J. EDWARDS,
      President of the Theological Seminary, Andover.

REV. SIR ;
      . . . The occasion naturally called for an exposition of my opinions with regard to the inconsistency between the principles asserted in the Declaration of Independence and the existence of Domestic slavery. I thought it also a fitting occasion to state the grounds of my belief that the ultimate extinguishment of slavery throughout the earth was the great transcendent earthly object of

[1] Diary XI, 341.

the mission of the Redeemer. . . . That the Declaration of Independence was a leading event in the progress of the gospel dispensation. . . . That its principles lead directly to the abolition of slavery and of war, and that it is the duty of every free American to contribute to the utmost extent of his power to the practical establishment of those principles. . . .

The difficulty which Mr. Adams encountered, in reducing his theory as a Christian, to practice may be stated in a nutshell, and the result to which it led him shall follow in his own words.

Mr. Adams as a scientific man was a precursor of the later Darwinians who have preached the doctrine of human perfectability, a doctrine in which the modern world has believed and still professes to believe. Granting that there is a benign and omnipotent Creator of the world, who watches over the fate of men, Adams' sincere conviction was that such a being thinks according to certain fixed laws, which we call scientific laws; that these laws may be discovered by human intelligence and when discovered may be adapted to human uses. And if so discovered, adapted, and practised they must lead men certainly to an approach to perfection, and more especially to the elimination of war and slavery. The theory was pleasing, and since the time of Mr. Adams it has been generally accepted as the foundation of Ameri-

can education and the corner stone of democracy. But
mark how far it led Mr. Adams astray in 1828, and how
at last it broke his heart. Eli Whitney's cotton gin was
certainly one of the most famous and successful of the
applications of science to a supremely bountiful gift of
God, in making American cotton serviceable and cheap
to the whole human race. But it propagated slavery,
it turned the fair state of Virginia into an enormous slave-
breeding farm, whence forty thousand blacks were
annually exported to the South, and thus inexorably
induced the Civil War; so with the public lands which
Mr. Adams would willingly have given his life to save
for his contemporaries and their posterity. Railroads
and canals raised the price of these lands by making
them accessible. And this is what Mr. Adams saw in
the House of Representatives in 1838, and this is his
comment on the humanizing effect of applied science.
It was the triumph of Benton and Jackson, of the very
essence of evil, over him. "The thirst of a tiger for
blood is the fittest emblem of the rapacity with which
the members of all the new states fly at the public lands.
The constituents upon whom they depend are all settlers,
or tame and careless spectators of the pillage. They are
themselves enormous speculators and land-jobbers. It
were a vain attempt to resist them here." This was

written on June 12, 1838, and thus had the bargain of Benton with the planters been consummated by means of applied science.[1] Such bargains were to have been anticipated and would have been taken as a matter of course by an ordinary political huckster, but Mr. Adams, though after his defeat in 1828 he did practically, as he states here, give up the contest, because he had ceased to believe that God supported him, never could nor ever did reconcile himself to the destiny which this betrayal by God entailed on the world.

Nevertheless, it was all the logical result of competition, of applied science, and of education as stimulating social ambition, and therefore greed. As an old man Mr. Adams sat in Congress and watched the competition between slave and free labor gathering the heat which presaged a convulsion, and he confessed to himself that "the conflict will be terrible." On the other hand he had loved his mother as he never loved another human being on the earth. Come what might he could not surrender his hope of immortality. To have been driven to such an admission would have killed him. This internal conflict forced him to seek to sustain his sinking faith by such pretences as he found at hand.

In 1843 he was old, and physical ailments were crowd-

---

[1] "Memoirs" lx. 235.

ing upon him.   Among the worst of these was catarrh,
or "tussis senilis" as he called it, which afflicted him
much.   One communion Sunday in March he was kept
at home by this cough, and he employed his time in re-
cording the following reflections upon his past life and
his present belief.   It seems hardly credible that a man
of his energy of mind should have admitted what a pang
so slight a disappointment, which at an earlier day he
would have ignored, actually gave him as he peered at
the end into the gate of death.

"I have this day been debarred by my disease [catarrh]
from the privilege of attendance upon public worship,
and felt it with deep mortification.   The time has been,
chiefly in foreign countries, when I have too long inter-
mitted the duty of that attendance.   Of this I charge
myself especially when in Holland, in Berlin, in St.
Petersburg, and last in France. . . .   For this I blame myself; but the importance of regular attendance upon the
duties of the Christian Sabbath in social communion has
impressed itself more deeply on my mind in proportion as
I have advanced in years.   I had neglected to become a
member of the church till after the decease of my father —
another omission which I now regret.   I have at all times
been a sincere believer in the existence of a Supreme
Creator of the world, of an immortal principle within

D

myself, responsible to that Creator for my conduct upon earth, and of the divine mission of the crucified Saviour, proclaiming immortal life and preaching peace on earth, good will to men, the natural equality of all mankind, and the law, 'Thou shalt love thy neighbor as thyself.' Of all these articles of faith, all resting upon the first, the existence of an Omnipotent Spirit, I entertain involuntary and agonizing doubts, which I can neither silence nor expel, and against which I need for my own comfort to be fortified and sustained by stated and frequent opportunities of receiving religious admonition and instruction. I feel myself to be a frequent sinner before God, and I need to be often admonished of it, and exhorted to virtue. . . . This forms a regular portion of my habits of life, and I cannot feel the privation of it without painful sensibility."[1]

Mr. Adams considered his life a failure; and from his point of view it was a failure; and in the same way and by a parity of reasoning Henry considered his life a failure, because he had not accomplished what at the outset he hoped. For example, John Quincy Adams wrote only a few days before the stroke of paralysis which ended his work: "If my intellectual powers had been such as have been sometimes committed by the Creator of

[1] Diary XI, 340, 341.

man to single individuals of the species, my diary would
have been, next to the Holy Scriptures, the most precious
and valuable book ever written by human hands, and I
should have been one of the greatest benefactors of my
country and of mankind. I would, by the irresistible
power of genius and the irrepressible energy of will and
the favor of Almighty God, have banished war and
slavery from the face of the earth forever. But the con-
ceptive power of mind was not conferred upon me by
my Maker, and I have not improved the scanty portion
of His gifts as I might and ought to have done." Then
he adds, "May I never . . . murmur at the dispensations
of Providence." In other words he was disappointed because he was not supernatural. And yet, as a matter of
fact, Mr. Adams had one of the most powerful scientific
minds of his age, and of this he has left a record in his
report on weights and measures. Among my father's
sons not one save Henry had any aptitude for science;
the others were ordinary lawyers or men of affairs, but
in Henry the instinct which he inherited from his grandfather showed itself strongly and early. Henry in one
of the most charming passages in his "Education" has
told us how one day in London in 1867, when he was not
yet thirty, Sir Charles Lyell asked him to review his
"Principles" for him in America, and afterward, in token

of his appreciation and gratification at Henry's work, left him his field compass. Now Sir Charles, whom I, as a child, very well remember as a dear friend of my mother, though a most amiable and delightful old gentleman, was by no means careless of his own reputation and was more particularly anxious to be well presented to the American public. Hence the compliment to Henry was the more flattering coming from so old a man, then standing at the apex of scientific fame, toward a young one who had as yet made not even a shadowy reputation in the literary world. Nor had Henry any education in geology save what he gave himself. But Sir Charles, to his great credit, recognized thus promptly Henry's intelligence and industry. How well the work was done any one may see by reading the paper in the *North American Review*. And so it was with John Quincy Adams from whom he inherited his talent.

CHAPTER II

The Heritage of Henry Adams

WHEN Mr. Adams returned home in 1817 to take charge of the State Department, he found a resolution of the Senate awaiting him dated March 3, 1817, directing the Secretary of State to "prepare and report to the Senate a statement relative to the regulations and standards for weights and measures in the several states, and relative to the proceedings in foreign countries, for establishing uniformity in weights and measures, together with " suggestions as to the course proper to be adopted by the United States.

Most Secretaries of State have been content to discharge, with what credit they might, the duties of the office, and have found those ample to absorb their energy, but Mr. Adams was a man of a different kidney, and an estimate by the youngest of his grandsons, who has himself become old, of the activities of his grandfather contrasts strangely with his ancestor's morbid depreciation of himself.

One of his expedients for finding time was to rise at four o'clock in the morning. With this explanation it may, perhaps, be easier to understand how he succeeded in writing his report while holding office as Secretary of State at a period of high pressure in public business. For it was during this interval that, among other things, the Monroe Doctrine was formulated, that Jackson nearly brought us into war with England by his execution of Arbuthnot and Ambrister, and that the despatch to Erving was written. And in those days Mr. Adams had little help even in the commonest drudgery. He had no private secretary, much less a stenographer. He wrote every word himself, often copying the more important papers with a hand palsied by writer's cramp. At last in October, 1819, he resolutely got to work. He was confronted with the resolution of the Senate directing the Secretary of State to report upon the action taken by other nations regarding weights and measures and to suggest a policy for the United States.

Mr. Adams had a peculiar mind. It concentrated slowly but when centred it acted with extreme intensity. Once absorbed he lapsed into a species of trance in which he forgot all else. But the transition from politics to science was slow and painful.

Among the responsibilities of government few are graver than the regulation of weights and measures, and this responsibility increases with every advance in trade, in wealth, in applied science, or in invention. The coinage is a matter of weights; trade turns on measures, while the standardization of machinery presupposes absolute accuracy of measurement. One of the chief glories of the French Revolution was the perfecting of the metric system. Now that the metric system has been long established we can with difficulty realize the confusion which its introduction caused. As Mr. Adams observed in his report: "The substitution of an entire new system of weights and measures, instead of one long established and in general use, is one of the most arduous exercises of legislative authority. There is indeed no difficulty in enacting and promulgating the law; but the difficulties of carrying it into execution are always great, and have often proved insuperable."

To a great degree the French have always found them so. To this day they have never succeeded in applying the decimal system to time. "Weights and measures may be ranked among the necessaries of life, to every individual of human society. They enter into the economical arrangements and daily concerns of every family. They are necessary to every occupation of human industry; to the distribution and security of every species of property; to every transaction of trade and commerce; to the labors of the husbandman; to the ingenuity of the artificer;

to the studies of the philosopher; to the researches of the antiquarian; to the navigation of the mariner, and the marches of the soldier; to all the exchanges of peace, and all the operations of war." Suddenly one of the chiefest of the family of nations shifted its standard, and forthwith all other nations sought an adjustment. They seek one still. Accordingly many governments appointed commissions of eminent scientists to report not only on the value of the metric system itself, but upon the means of reaching a common standard. And these problems have never yet been satisfactorily solved. Parliament early bestirred itself, Congress somewhat later. And this was the resolve which awaited Mr. Adams after an absence of eight years. He had no commission with its resources at command. He was absolutely isolated and alone, and besides he found the Department itself in chaos. The confusion was in part due to the sack of Washington, but still more to the slackness which had prevailed from the foundation of the government in the filing of correspondence. Plunged forthwith in the Spanish turmoil which lasted from the occupation of Amelia Island in 1817, to the revolution which provoked the Monroe Doctrine, Mr. Adams passed much of his time in hunting for essential documents, and every practical man will sympathize with his nervous irritation at the strain put

upon him by having to teach his clerks some rudiments
of order, at the same time that he had to rout bitter ad-
versaries in front, and strengthen timid colleagues behind.   Doing, besides his own work as Secretary, that of
a common clerk, he was at the mercy of such an uncon-
scionable bore as the British Minister, Stratford Canning,
who thought nothing of idling away three or four hours
of a morning, at the Secretary's expense.

After his vacation in the summer of 1819, Mr. Adams
returned to Washington in October and resolutely attacked
his report.   Probably no political conflict in which he ever
engaged wrought his nerves to so high a tension, for in
science he entered into, as it were, a foreign field and one in
which he felt much diffidence, as was reasonable, for the
difficulties he encountered might have discouraged the best
trained mathematician and physicist in the world.   Working under the best conditions with every appliance and
vast libraries at hand, the combined talent of France
and England had reached no satisfactory conclusion
touching the relation of the foot to the metre.   And
Adams had to criticise the discrepancies between the
various measurements of the British pendulum vibrating
seconds in vacuo.   The difference according to him between a committee of the House of Commons and Cap-
tain Kater was an one hundred and twenty-sixth part

of an inch. Thus even in London or Paris the investigator had much to contend with, but without doubt no considerable capital in the civilized world was so bereft of experimental appliances as was then Washington, which was little better than a poorly administered southern village, with all the educational slackness which that implies. Nor had Adams the training or experience to be able to make good these deficiencies from his own resources. Even his mathematics he had to furbish up as he went along. In science he was self-educated. He could neither invent new apparatus, nor repair injured pieces. Hardly could he command the use of a chronometer. Worst of all, he found no kindred mind from which he could draw a stimulant. Nor could he give to his work either the best of his time during the day or the best days of the year. The only hours he could veritably call his own were from three o'clock in the morning until breakfast, and those only in summer, in hot weather, when work was fatiguing almost beyond endurance. In winter social engagements at night prevented him from rising so early, and visits at the office effectually put a stop to serious concentration during the day. Therefore to work consecutively he had to give up his visit to his father at Quincy in August, which almost broke the poor old man's heart, after his wife had died, as occurred long before 1819. And thus John Quincy Adams passed all summer laboriously writing in Washington, though writing had become beyond measure irksome to him in the moist heat of the Potomac Valley, which always debilitated him.

For months his diary is filled with plaints about the pressure on his time, and the misery of trying to concentrate his attention in Washington in summer, and with strange accounts of the rude experiments to which he was constrained to resort to test his theories. For example, one set of his instruments was an old pair of bank scales "which belonged to the Branch of the old Bank of the United States, but which having been disused are not regulated and have grown rusty."

Another time he was quite at a loss to find out the content of an ordinary hogshead of Bordeaux. In hardly any other city in the world would he have had to do more than to ask at the chief grocer's counter, but in Washington nobody knew. These daily incidents illustrate the shifts to which he was driven.

The whole diary is filled for months with entries which would be of absorbing interest to any reader who wished to measure the natural scientific powers of my grandfather but which would be misplaced here. I am engaged not in writing a biography of John Quincy Adams but in making only such a statement of the temperament of the man as may serve to elucidate the actions and writings of one of his grandsons as well as his own. Hence, I must pass over the details of the composition of the Report, and hasten at once to its publication.

As the month of October, 1820, wasted, Mr. Adams' anxiety to finish it became so acute that he suffered severely from insomnia, and yet in spite of all obstacles, even of Stratford Canning, who lounged in the office at the rate of three hours a day and then insulted the Secretary, thereby throwing a mass of additional copying on his hands, Adams succeeded in sending his report to Congress on February 22, 1821. This was also the day on which the Florida treaty was ratified, which Mr. Adams held to be his great diplomatic triumph.

At the moment of publication Mr. Adams felt abashed, as it was reasonable that an essentially modest man, like himself, should feel, for though he knew that he had done his best, he dared not hope that he had made good his deficiencies, and he saw no one to whom he could turn for criticism or for aid in his perplexities. Before the final revision, indeed, he sent the copy to Calhoun, who, while generally approving, suggested a few slight alterations and omissions, all of which Adams adopted. But Calhoun was by no means an authority on science.

And "who was he," as Adams told himself despondently, to venture to expound, "a subject which has occupied for the last sixty years many of the ablest men in Europe, and to which all the power and all the philosophical and mathematical learning and ingenuity of France and Great Britain have been incessantly directed?" At first the scientific world was inclined to take him at his own valuation. No trade or profession likes interlopers, science, perhaps, least of all, and so far as immediate success went, Mr. Adams' very strength militated most strongly against him. Science could not believe that it could be sound and yet literary, artistic, and historical. A man who produced a gem like the Report of Weights and Measures must necessarily be a quack. For the Report on Weights and Measures is a vast effort at generalization. It was unprecedented. It deals with history and philosophy quite as much as with physics. Richard Rush, who was very intelligent, laid his finger instantly upon the weak spot. "I have finished a first perusal of the report on weights and mesures and must say, with far more interest than I ever expected to feel in the pursuit of such a discussion. . . . Of its various scientific deductions, I am no judge, but naturally place these at a high rate from the abundant research of which the investigation everywhere bears evidence. It is not always that elaborate deductions of science, come recommended by so much literature and eloquence. I have always thought the subject dry, but I see that it is most fruitful; I had thought it circumscribed, but I see that it embraces everything."

As Rush intimated the Report was too broad for any contemporary audience. It contained too much science for the general public, and too much literature for the profession. Science always tends to a narrow specialization. Mathematicians in especial distrust inferences based on premises drawn from history or philosophy. Conversely Rush said bluntly that his opinion on the technical side was worthless. And yet it was upon its technical excellence that the work must stand or fall. Precisely in the same way, John Adams, who would have devoured with ravenous relish every word his beloved son might have chanced to write on jurisprudence, metaphysics, politics, or history, had to admit that he could not read physics, so widely were their minds sundered on this subject which he had never studied and for which he had no aptitude.

LITTLE HILL, MAY 10, 1821.

MY DEAR SON ;

My thanks are due to you, and are most joyfully given, for two copies of your "Report on Weights and Meas-

ures," . . . Though I cannot say, and perhaps shall
never be able to say, that I have read it, yet I have turned
over leaves of it enough to see that it is a mass of historical, philosophical, chemical, metaphysical and political knowledge, which no industry in this country but
yours could have collected in so short a time. . . .   Washington used to say sometimes, "They work me hard."
I am sure they work you harder, I fear they will work you
up too soon.   I am glad to perceive that your brother
[Thomas Adams, the judge of the Court of Common
Pleas], is reading the book with attention.

The poor old man loathed the Report for it kept his son
in Washington whom he was wearing his heart out to see,
and so the letter ended, with a prayer for pity; "I long to
see you once more and hope for that pleasure as soon as the
public service will permit, I subscribe with pride and
exquisite delight, your affectionate father."   In America
the work fell dead.   That it should have done so was to
be expected since literary suspicion and incredulity of
compatriots is a national quality.   We have never overcome that trait of provincialism.   For an American
author to receive credit in his own country, he must
first win reputation abroad.   Thus it happened in the
case of Mr. Adams.   He obtained no word of intelligent
criticism until, thirteen years after the book had been
published, he made the following entry in his diary,
touching a letter which had reached him in Quincy from

one Colonel Pasley, of the Royal Engineers, who had himself been publishing a work on Weights and Measures.
He "says he has done justice to my report made to the
Senate of the United States in 1821, acknowledging that
my historical account of English Weights and Measures
is more correct than any that has been given by any
English writer, including the reports of the committees
of the House of Commons. This acknowledgment, thirteen years after the publication of my report, was very
gratifying to me. If either of my children or any of theirs
should ever read this page, let me tell him that Colonel
Pasley's testimonial to that single point, the accuracy
of my historical investigation of English weights and
measures, is but one of many discoveries which he will
find in my report, if he will have the courage and persever-
ance to read, and examine it as he reads. He will find
the history not only of English but of Hebrew, Greek,
Roman, and French weights and measures, traced to their
origin, in the natural history of man and of human society,
such as he can find in no other writer, ancient or modern.

" He will find a philosophical discussion of the moral
principles involved in the consideration of weights and
measures, and of the extent and limitation of its connection
with binal, decimal, and duodecimal arithmetic, for which
he might look in vain elsewhere ; and if he should remark

that not one of his countrymen ever noticed these peculiarities of that report, he may amuse himself by in-
quiring why and how it has happened. The report, from
the day of its publication, has, in this country, scarcely
been known to exist; and this commendation of it,
coming back from England, is, therefore, the more welcome to me." [1]

Mr. Adams apparently intended to intimate to us, his
descendants, that we should do well to be modest in our
expectations if we looked for recognition for anything
which we might produce containing original ideas, or
attempts at generalization. For what he says of himself is true. His work of weights and measures is monumental and has, since his death, been so recognized by a
younger generation who did not feel themselves to be in
competition with him. But the scientific is like any
other profession, it looks with jealousy on an interloper,
who undertakes to generalize from premises of which
scientific men are perhaps ignorant. For, as a rule, no
scientist pretends to know much history. Once, however, that the value of the report had been demonstrated ample recognition came.

Twenty-one years after its author's death, Professor
Charles Davies, who long had been eminent, and who

[1] Diary IX, 185.

E

for many years had filled the chair of mathematics at Columbia and at West Point, was appointed by a committee of the University Convocation of the State of New York, to examine into the policy of Congress in enacting a statute in 1866 making the metric system lawful in the United States. Professor Davies passed two years in investigation himself, and then submitted his report in the form of a volume of three hundred and twenty-seven pages, divided into four parts. To part three of this exhaustive work he prefixed the following introduction which is the more remarkable, as few scientific works retain their value, as text-books, very long. This was written fifty years after publication.

"Part III. is the able and extraordinary report of Mr. John Quincy Adams. He examined the whole subject with the minuteness and accuracy of mathematical science — with the keen sagacity of statesmanship, and the profound wisdom of philosophy. To that report nothing can be added, and from it nothing should be taken away. Hence the committee have published it in full, that the public and especially the teachers of the country, may understand the entire subject in all its phases and in all its relations."

Another quarter of a century elapsed, and in 1906, Sir Sandford Flemming, as chairman of a committee appointed by the Royal Society of Canada to consider the forty-inch metre, on May 25, presented a report accompanied by an address in which after observing that "International uniformity in weights and measures has been desired for many generations," went on to cite the opinions of several eminent philosophers. The first among these to whom Sir Sandford referred was John Quincy Adams.

"Among the many distinguished men who within the last hundred years have studied the question with the view of finding a solution to the important international problem was John Quincy Adams, who three years before he became the sixth president of the United States drew up a report on weights and measures which is still a classic, and shows an almost incredible amount of investigation."

Finally, in 1906, Messrs. Hallock and Wade published an elaborate work on the "Evolution of Weights and Measures," presumably, considering the high reputation of these gentlemen, containing the maturest conclusions of modern science. In this work the authors devote some considerable space to the report of John Quincy Adams, with whose conclusions they disagree. Their criticism, nevertheless, begins thus: "Adams . . . submitted [a report] on February 22, 1821, that has since been

considered almost a classic in American metrology. . . .
While it is, of course, impossible to do justice to the
completeness and philosophic treatment of the subject
in this report, by any summary or brief extracts, nevertheless a few passages will show how keen was Mr. Adams'
understanding of the matter, and how well he appreciated
the advantages of the French system."[1]

Precisely in the same way I have some reason to expect
that much of the scientific world will sneer at Henry's
inferences in "Phase." And in publishing his essay I
give full weight to my grandfather's warning to expect
nothing.

But touching John Quincy Adams, from whom Henry
received so abundant a share of his inheritance of intellectual capacity, science was his tenderest part, and
the part where he received the least sympathy and intelligent support from his family or friends. Henry has
told us how at Quincy no one took the old man's garden-
ing seriously, and in the country at large his luck was
little better, and this tried him, perhaps more than all
the rest. For example, when president, he observed
how the live-oak was wasted and abused and he attempted

[1] " Outlines of the Evolution of Weights and Measures and the Metric
System, by William Hallock, Professor of Physics in Columbia Uni-
versity, and Herbert T. Wade, Editor for Physics and Applied Science,
The New International Encyclopedia," pp. 115, 116.

to protect it. In 1828 he matured a plan to preserve a forest of live-oak near Pensacola, because the natural history of the live-oak had many singularities and had not been observed; and this plantation was growing luxuriantly, and numbered upwards of a hundred thousand trees, to which he added a nursery of seedlings that their habits might be observed. All this, as Adams bitterly observed afterward, "is to be abandoned by the stolid ignorance and stupid malignity of John Branch and of his filthy subaltern, Amos Kendall." He could not reconcile himself "to the malicious pleasure of [Jackson's administration,] of destroying everything of which I had planted the germ."

With Mr. Adams science and education were passions, and amounted to a religion, as I have said. For forty years ago the theory of progression towards perfection was popularly accepted as Henry has described it to have been in his "Education." "Unbroken Evolution under uniform conditions pleased every one, — except curates and bishops; it was the very best substitute for religion."[1] All of which was perfectly true of London in the sixties, but it was not thus that John Quincy Adams mingled his science with his God. To him the issue was, literally, one of life and death, for were his premises false, and were he

[1] "Education," 225.

mistaken in his belief that the universe were ruled by a conscious and benign God, then progressive improvement would be impossible, civilization would be a failure, and the world itself a place in which he cared not to live.

Never was crusader more sternly in earnest in his belief in the miraculous virtue of the relics which he had suffered so much to conquer and by which he hoped to gain felicity on earth and in heaven, than was John Quincy Adams in 1828 in his faith that there was a God in heaven whose thought was manifested in those truths which he described as scientific laws, which would, were they properly studied and observed, certainly lead to such an approach to perfection as would enable mankind to suppress forever the ulcers of war and slavery.

Doubtless as the election of 1828 approached he had his fears. He mistrusted himself as to whether he had duly served his Creator. But he never suspected that God could not cause him to triumph if he would. In the same way, Guy de Lusignan with his crusaders fought Saladin at Tiberias in 1187, in the faith that the cross they bore before them would give them victory, if only God would work his miracle. Both believers were totally defeated and the effect on their world was much the same. After Tiberias the relics lost their value, so much so that from having been accepted as the best possible security for loans by bankers, they fell to the point where they became an absolute danger to the possessor, as the monks found to their cost in England in the sixteenth century. Adams did not fare quite so badly as did the wretched Abbot of Glastonbury under Henry VIII, but he suffered enough to embitter him permanently and to make him seriously doubt the existence of a God and of the efficacy of science as a guide. Nevertheless he persevered to the end of his life, always hoping against hope. To him the alternative was too dreadful for contemplation. It so happened that in October of 1830 his neighbors of the Plymouth District nominated Mr. Adams for Congress, and in the following November they elected him by a great majority. On the evening of November 6, the day on which he heard the news, he sat alone at home, meditating on what had befallen him. The event to him was quite unexpected. It fairly bewildered him. He thus poured out his feelings: "Twenty-two towns gave 2565 votes, of which 1817 were for John Quincy Adams. . . . I am a member elect of the Twenty-Second Congress. . . . My return to public life in a subordinate station is disagreeable to my family, and disapproved by some of my friends; though no one has expressed that disapprobation to me.

" For the discharge of the duties of this particular station

I never was eminently qualified, possessing no talent for extemporaneous public speaking, and at this time being in the decline of my faculties, both of mind and body. This event, therefore, gives me deep concern and anxious forebodings . . . No one knows, and few conceive, the agony of mind that I have suffered from the time that I was made by circumstances, and not by my volition, a candidate for the presidency till I was dismissed from that station by the failure of my reëlection. They were feelings to be suppressed and they were suppressed. No human being has ever heard me complain. . . .

"But this call upon me by the people of the district in which I reside, to represent them in Congress, has been spontaneous, and although counteracted by a double opposition, federalist and Jacksonite, I have received nearly three votes in four throughout the district. My election as President of the United States was not half so gratifying to my inmost soul. No election or appointment conferred upon me ever gave me so much pleasure. I say this to record my sentiments; but no stranger intermeddleth with my joys, and the dearest of my friends have no sympathy with my sensations."

Yet almost incredible as it may seem, despite his misgivings, Mr. Adams after taking his seat in Congress, though opposed through the remainder of his life by a series of democratic administrations and by a reactionary, victorious, and malignant slave oligarchy, succeeded rather better as a lonely member of the House in the advancement of those ideas which he considered that he had been born to preach, than he had as President of the United States, with all the power and influence which that office gives.

Certainly toward the end of his life he exercised a far greater influence on popular opinion than he had ever attained to before. Inside of Congress and out, he toiled unceasingly to improve education and to stimulate science. He urged on Congress the organization of a naval academy to train men of the quality of his contemporaries, Maury, Gilliss, and Davis, and he never remitted his agitation for an observatory. In his vacations he experimented on tree planting and lectured on education. In New York and Philadelphia he attended conventions of learned societies, and he so impressed himself on those with whom he came in contact, that he finally made even a slave-holding Congress recognize his ability and use him whenever they thought it safe to do so.

Occasionally scientific matters came before Congress when special committees were appointed and then the speaker not infrequently appointed Adams chairman, when he seldom failed to offer some suggestion of appropriations and to sustain them with a luminous report. An example of such a paper is the report he made in 1840 on a petition of the American Philosophical Society, headed by Bache, asking for magnetic observatories. But his most brilliant service in this connection was his defence of the Smithson bequest. In 1826 James Smithson bequeathed £100,000 to the United States, to found in Washington, under the name of the Smithsonian Institution, an establishment for the "increase and diffusion of knowledge among men." Finally, after the death of Mr. Smithson in 1835, through the services of Mr. Rush, £104,599 in gold were brought home and in 1838 were deposited in the mint in Philadelphia, and then at once an acrimonious controversy touching the execution of the trust set in, fomented by every adventurer in search of a job in the United States. The struggle lasted several years, and meanwhile the only practical step the government took was, as a popular measure, to invest the whole fund in Arkansas bonds, which proved to be worthless. Mr. Adams, as chairman of the House Committee, made a series of reports, the most famous of which is that of 1840, in which he presented resolutions pledging the United States to preserve the principal of the bequest unimpaired and so invested as to yield six per cent, while the income of the fund alone should be used for the objects of the bequest.   Mr. Adams advised that the first appropriation should be for the establishment of an observatory.   Other reports of the same character followed.   So full of vigor are these papers that Professor Nourse, the historian of the Naval Observatory, observes in his memoir, published in 1873, alluding to the report of 1842, "The remark has been made by a competent judge that it is 'well worth the perusal of every lover of the glorious science of astronomy, both for the richness of its information and the beauty of its eloquence.' " [1]

Finally even so reactionary a body as an American Congress, dominated by slave-holders, perceived that an observatory was an essential part of the equipment of any civilized government and took steps to build one at Washington.   Needless to say this plan was enthusiastically approved by Mr. Adams, but years were still to elapse before his anxieties were to cease and his labors were to be crowned with success touching the Smithsonian. Nevertheless, among all Mr. Adams' scientific interests astronomy stirred him most, and an attempt to stimulate that branch of science finally cost him his life.   When he described his emotions on contemplating the heavens, he sometimes used language of great imaginative power.

[1] Memoir of the Founding and Progress of the United States Naval Observatory, Professor J. E. Nourse, U. S. N. p. 25.

"To me, the observation of the sun, moon, and stars has been for a great portion of my life a pleasure of gratified curiosity, of ever returning wonder, and of reverence for the Creator and mover of these unnumbered worlds. There is something of awful enjoyment in observing the rising and setting of the sun. That flashing beam of his first appearance upon the horizon; that sinking of the last ray beneath it; that perpetual revolution of the Great and Little Bear round the pole; that rising of the whole constellation of Orion from the horizontal to the perpendicular position, and his ride through the heavens, with his belt, his nebulous sword, and his four corner stars of the first magnitude, are sources of delight to me which never tire. . . . There is, indeed, intermingled with all this a painful desire to know more of this stupendous system; of sorrow in reflecting how little we can ever know of it; and of almost desponding hope that we may know more of it hereafter." [1]

Thus astronomy appealed to Mr. Adams both through the imagination and the reason, and he concluded, and probably correctly, that astronomy would be the best instrument wherewith to rouse to an interest in science a somewhat apathetic community. Up to 1844 the United States did not possess a single observatory. Mariners

[1] X, 38.

had to depend upon the calculations made at Greenwich. A nautical almanac was impossible. Even the longitude of Washington could not be fixed with proper exactness, and this inertia filled Mr. Adams with shame. In his first message to Congress he urged the erection of an observatory in words which filled the friends of General Jackson with mirth.

"It is with no feeling of pride as an American, that the remark may be made, that, on the comparatively small territorial surface of Europe, there are existing more than one hundred and thirty of these light-houses of the skies; while throughout the whole American hemisphere there is not one." The phrase "light-houses of the skies" probably brought more ridicule on Mr. Adams than anything he ever said. The line which divided John Quincy Adams from even the most enlightened of his political contemporaries was most distinctly his aptitude for science. He alone among public men of that period appreciated that a nation to flourish under conditions of modern economic competition, must organize its administrative, as well as its social system upon scientific principles.

Years elapsed, and Mr. Adams grew old. Apparently he had achieved little toward realizing his dream of doing a work beneficial to mankind. He had been defeated in his effort to organize the national administration of public affairs upon a scientific basis, he had failed to accomplish anything of moment by his experiments in cultivation at Quincy, he had indeed been greatly ridiculed even in his family; he had not even been able to induce Congress to execute honestly its trust relative to the Smithsonian bequest, but he had won renown as an antislavery champion. His fame and popularity were astounding.

CHAPTER III

THE HERITAGE OF HENRY ADAMS

IN July, 1843, he happened to take a vacation journey to Niagara with Mr. Brooks and my mother. Hardly had he entered the state of New York when this journey was transformed into a triumphal progress by a spontaneous popular ovation. In the midst of the outburst, on July 24, while at Niagara, Professor Mitchel arrived from Cincinnati, bringing an invitation from an astronomical society organized there, to deliver an oration at the laying of the corner-stone of the observatory they were about to build. Mr. Adams immediately became much excited. "I asked Mr. Mitchel for a short interval of time to make up my mind upon a proposal so strange to me; and so flattering that I scarcely dare to think of it with composure." The next day he accepted. Probably he never thought seriously of declining, and yet he knew the risks he ran, and the remote possibility of advantage to himself. Perhaps of English and American statesmen, situated as he was then situated, Bacon and Franklin alone might have taken the view he took and chosen as he chose. Hardly could he justify himself in his own eye. "I have accepted the invitation, and promised to perform the

duty, if in my power, on some day in the month of
November next. . . . This is a rash promise, and, in faithfully analyzing my motives for making it, I wish I could
find them pure from all alloy of vanity and self-glorifi-
cation. It is an arduous, hazardous, and expensive undertaking, the successful performance of which is more than
problematical, and of the event of which it is impossible
for me to foresee anything but disappointment. Yet,
there is a motive pure and elevated, and a purpose benevolent and generous, at least, mingling with the impulses
which in this case I obey." [1]

On July 25, 1843, when John Quincy Adams wrote
these words, he had entered upon his seventy-seventh
year. The ceremony was to take place the following
November. He had then held almost every office in the
gift of the people or of the government. In his old age,
after a life of turmoil and of alternations of fortunes, he
had reached the pinnacle of dignity and of honor. His
constitution though relatively vigorous had been strained
by his labors ; he suffered from a bad catarrhal cough
aggravated by excessive public speaking ; he could not
fill a tithe of the calls upon him made imperative by his
position as a political leader. He stood in much need of
repose before the next session of Congress would begin.

[1] XI, 394, 5.

If he accepted the invitation, he must prepare an oration which should be worthy of the occasion and of himself, he must face a journey of great hardship, in an inclement season, and he must undergo the fatigue of a prolonged public ovation, an ordeal which always filled him with dismay.   So far as he could then see, he could gain nothing personally, save the slight satisfaction of linking his name with the foundation of the first American observatory, a fact which would be soon forgotten.   On the other hand, he might use his fleeting popularity to promote science. This consideration prevailed.   He determined to make the effort, and run the risk.   The risk proved to be greater than even he supposed.   From the fatigue and exposure of that journey he never fully recovered, and as the point whence Mr. Adams began rapidly to fail, the Cincinnati celebration has a pathetic interest.   The strain told almost immediately. Mr. Adams had never known popularity, and his journey through New York wrought upon him.   His nerves had lost their elasticity, and excitement made him sleepless.   Worst of all, although oppressed with work, he found he could no longer labor as had been his wont.

As the weeks passed he found himself less and less able to cope with his accumulating tasks.   He could not escape meeting his constituents before leaving home for

F

the winter, and by September 7, he complained that arrears of correspondence and his address oppressed him "to distraction." On September 20, he was persuaded to consent to lecture at Springfield on his way to the west, and the excitement and worry of these "manifold engagements" produced serious insomnia. "A state of existence bordering I fear upon insanity, and which I contemplate with alarm." [1]

Meanwhile he toiled on his oration, which he hoped to make a history of astronomy so alluring that it would kindle lasting enthusiasm. Every library, public and private, within reach was put under contribution, and his friends journeyed to Quincy laden with books. He dwelt much in secret on what he hoped to accomplish; he recognized that this was the last opportunity he should ever have to realize his aspiration of stimulating his generation to intellectual activity. "My task is to turn this transient gust of enthusiasm for the science of astronomy at Cincinnati into a permanent and persevering national pursuit, which may extend the bounds of human knowledge, and make my country instrumental in elevating the character and improving the condition of man upon earth. The hand of God himself has furnished me this opportunity to do good. But Oh! how much will

[1] MSS. Sept. 21, 1843.

depend upon my manner of performing that task! And
with what agony of soul must I implore the aid of Almighty Wisdom for powers of conception, energy of exer-
tion, and unconquerable will to accomplish my design." [1]
I think he never wrote with such intensity of feeling of
any political event.

On October 20, at eleven o'clock at night, perforce he
brought his oration "to a sudden and abrupt termination."
There was no time for revision. It was only possible
with haste to have a single copy made. He admitted
to himself that he "shivered at the thought." His
departure was then only three days distant, and one of
those days had to be devoted to the meeting at Dedham.
As his departure approached, his friends were appalled
at the thought of the journey and of the fatigue. In his
journal he has related how Mr. Thayer called upon
him "and was quite discomposed at the prospect of my
expedition — and foresees from it nothing but disaster to
myself." Then as always Mr. Adams admitted that he
might have been rash, but that it was too late to reconsider,
— "I must go happen what may."

Tuesday, October 24, was his last day at home. Having
worked till one o'clock in the morning on his speech to
his constituents, he rose at half past four to go to Dedham.

[1] Memoirs, 19 Sept., 1843.

The whole country side thronged to hear him. A caval-cade met him. The church was packed. He spoke two hours and a half. "A miserable fragment," as he thought, "of what it should have been." The next morning after snatching something to eat at quarter past five, he drove to the station in Boston, and took the train for Springfield, where he was to lecture. On reaching Springfield, "I was so worn down with weariness, three almost sleepless nights and anxiety, that my faculties seemed benumbed, and I felt as if falling into a lethargy."

At Springfield the weather turned cold. In crossing the river at Albany "I felt as if I were incrusted in a bed of snow." In the morning he was awakened by the hail. The train was frozen to the rails, and could not be broken free for an hour. At Buffalo his accommodation was wretched, and on Lake Erie he met a fierce snow storm, and was wind-bound for a day and a half, "as cold as Nova Zembla." At Cleveland a choice had to be made between travelling night and day by stage coach over two hundred and thirty miles of bad and dangerous roads to Columbus, or four days by canal boat, on the Ohio Canal. Those in charge of his journey chose the boat, but before departing he had been recognized in a barber shop, and had to undergo a reception.

In the afternoon he went on board the canal boat very

unwell with catarrh, sore throat, and fever. The boat was eighty feet long, and fifteen feet wide, and besides his own party was packed with the crew, four horses, and twenty other passengers. "So much humanity crowded into such a compass was a trial such as I had never before experienced, and my heart sunk within me when, squeezing into this pillory, I reflected that I am to pass three nights and four days in it." — " We were obliged to keep the windows of the cabins closed against the driving snow, and the stoves heated with billets of wood, made the rooms uncomfortably warm." "About eleven o'clock I took to my settee bed, with a head-ache, feverish chills, hoarseness, and a sore throat, and my 'tussis senilis' in full force." He lay in a compartment "with an iron stove in the centre, and side settees, on which four of us slept, feet to feet," next to "a bulging stable" for the horses.

Moving at about two miles and a half an hour, bumping into all the innumerable locks, until the boat "staggers along like a stumbling nag," Mr. Adams sometimes tried to write amidst babel, and sometimes played euchre, of which he had never heard before. At each town where they stopped there was a reception, handshaking, and speeches. On November 4, the party reached Columbus, where a committee of the Astronomical Society were in waiting, but his cough increased in severity, and the throng of visitors was overwhelming. At Jefferson and Springfield the same scenes were repeated, and he entered Dayton "in triumphal procession," and found "a vast multitude of the people assembled" before the hotel. Mr. Adams had to speak from a barouche. "I was beset the whole evening by a succession of visitors in squads, to be introduced and shake hands, to every one of whom I was a total stranger, and the name of not one of whom I can remember. My friends Grinnell and W. C. Johnson give me every possible encouragement in getting along; but the strangeness of these proceedings increases like a ball of snow. I cannot realize that these demonstrations are made for me; and the only comfort I have is that they are intended to manifest respect, and not hatred."[1] Far from home, in the middle of winter, the old man realized that he was breaking down.

At Lebanon the famous Thomas Corwin welcomed him before an enormous audience in "an address of splendid eloquence." Mr. Adams was covered with confusion.

"These premeditated addresses by men of the most consummate ability, and which I am required to answer off hand, without an instant for reflection, are distressing beyond measure and humiliating to agony."[2] He "re-

[1] XI, 423.   [2] XI, 424.

tired worn out with fatigue." The tact of his friends, who probably perceived his condition, somewhat allevi- ated his misery, "but my catarrh and excessive kind- ness drive me to despair." [1] At Cincinnati, there were more processions, more crowds, and another open-air address delivered from the balcony of the hotel, in re- sponse to the welcome of the mayor. "My answer was flat, stale, and unprofitable, without a spark of eloquence or a flash of oratory, confused, incoherent, muddy, and yet received with new shouts of welcome." At Cincinnati also he heard from the committee on arrangements that he was to deliver an address on the spot where the stone was laid, as well as the oration. This address was unexpected and of course unprepared. He had to write it at night.

"Worn down with fatigue, anxiety and shame, as I was, and with the oppression of a catarrhal load upon my lungs, I sat up till one in the morning, writing the address, which, from utter exhaustion, I left unfinished, and retired to a sleepless bed. I fear I am not duly grateful to Divine Providence for the blessing of these demonstrations of kindness and honor from my countrymen." The next day it rained in torrents. It rained so hard that it wet through the manuscript from which Mr. Adams read

[1] XI, 425.

when the stone was laid, and the oration had to be deferred. He finally delivered it on November 10, in the largest church in the city, crowded to suffocation. Mr. Adams then spoke for about two hours, as he observed with satisfaction, without a "symptom of impatience or inattention" among the audience. There was good reason for attention. An intelligent audience could hardly have been inattentive, for the oration is a gem. It can still be read with delight, although it bears the marks of the pressure under which it was written. Its arrangement is defective and its termination abrupt, but notwithstanding these defects it probably remains the most compact, suggestive, and imaginative essay upon astronomy, in the language. Had the author enjoyed the strength and leisure to revise it, it would have taken its place as a classic beside the "Weights and Measures."

Receptions awaited him as he ascended the Ohio, the last of which, at Pittsburg, he found "inexpressibly irksome." "These mass meetings, at which I find myself held up as a show, where the most fulsome adulation is addressed to me face to face in the presence of thousands, — all this is so adverse to my nature that . . . I am like one coming out of a trance or fainting fit, unconscious of what has been passing around me." [1]

[1] XI, 438.

From Pittsburg he travelled by stage coach to Cumberland, the weather was excessively cold, and on leaving Pittsburg on November 21, he admitted to himself that he was dangerously ill. "The stamina of my constitution are sinking under the hardships and exposures of travelling at this season and at my time of life. . . . My racking cough all last night left me scarce an hour of sleep, and no repose. I was up at three and again at four, and wrote on the arrears of this diary from that time till seven."

At Union-town "I passed a night of torture, with a hacking and racking cough, and feverish headache. I went to bed at 9, and was up with fits of coughing at 11, at 1, at 3, and at 5 this morning, and finally lay till near 6 utterly dispirited." Sixty-two miles of hard stage riding over the national road lay between him and Cumberland. "My expedient to husband my strength till I can get home is abstinence . . . I ate nothing the whole day." [1]

What impression John Quincy Adams made upon the philosophical and educational tendencies of his generation cannot be determined, but probably he acted powerfully upon his age. Astronomy, for example, which in 1825 was the laughing stock of Congress, became before his death the pampered pet of the nation. Certainly no

[1] MS. 22 Nov., 1843.

American statesman, save Franklin, has done more for science.

Nevertheless men seldom attain precisely that for which they strive by the means they use; ordinarily the result of their efforts differs from their anticipation. It may have been so with Mr. Adams touching this Cincinnati journey. He risked his life to stimulate science. Perhaps in this direction he may have accomplished less than he had hoped, but the political effect of his astounding progress through Ohio was prodigious. He left Congress a radical whom the conservatives had narrowly failed to expel. He returned a broken old man, but one before whom the South quailed. He had no illusions. He frankly admitted to himself that, in substance, he had committed suicide for the sake of science. He wrote on the day on which he passed his own door, November 24, 1843: "I have performed my task, I have executed my undertaking, and am returned safe to my family and my home. It is not much in itself. It is nothing in the estimation of the world. In my motives and my hopes, it is considerable. The people of this country do not sufficiently estimate the importance of patronizing and promoting science as a principle of political action; and the slave oligarchy systematically struggle to suppress all public patronage or countenance to the progress of the mind. Astronomy has been especially neglected and scornfully treated. This invitation had a gloss of showy representation about it that wrought more on the public mind than many volumes of dissertation or argument. I hoped to draw a lively and active attention to it among the people, and to put in motion a propelling power of intellect which will no longer stagnate into rottenness. I indulge dreams of future improvement to result from this proclamation of popular homage to the advancement of science . . . But I return to my home with the symptoms of speedy dissolution upon me. I had no conception of the extent to which I have been weakened by this tussis senilis, . . . or old man's cough. My strength is prostrated beyond anything that I ever experienced before, even to total impotence. I have little life left in me." To this sentence my father has appended this note. "There can be little doubt that this statement is substantially true. Mr. Adams had much overtaxed his physical powers in this trip." My grandmother was aghast when she saw him. On the 25th, one day later, she wrote to my father, "Your father, my dear Charles, has returned in a state of debility and exhaustion beyond description." She called in the family physician who, she reported, thought his symptoms "very dangerous," and she begged my father to visit her friend, Dr. Jacob

Bigelow, and ask him to send immediately "a few lines intimating the necessity of prudence," or her husband's impatience of control might be fatal. But it was of no avail. John Quincy Adams perfectly appreciated his predicament and what he had deliberately done. He was unrepentant. Had the opportunity been open to him to roll time backward like Hezekiah on the dial of Ahaz, and to re-live his visit to Niagara, knowing all that had happened, his choice would still have been the same. The only reply he made to his wife when she pleaded with him was: "It would be a glorious moment for me to die, so let it come." And it did come.

On August 15, 1846, he returned to Quincy from Washington. The next morning was Sunday, and on waking he wrote the following species of supplication or prayer which is, in effect, his farewell to life.

"Quincy, Sunday, August 16th, 1846. — Blessing, praise, and supplication to God on first rising from bed on returning to my earthly home, after an absence of nine months in the public service of my country. Some discouragement of soul follows the reflection that my aspirations to live in the memory of after-ages as a benefactor of my country and of mankind have not received the sanction of my Maker; that the longing of my soul through a long life to be numbered among the blessings bestowed by the Creator on the race of man is rejected; and after being trammelled and counteracted and disabled at every step of my progress, my faculties are now declining from day to day into mere helpless impotence. Yet at the will of my heavenly Father why should I repine?"

Like Moses, and a host of other idealists and reformers, John Quincy Adams had dreamed that, by his interpretation of the divine thought, as manifested in nature, he could covenant with God, and thus regenerate mankind. He knew that he had kept his part of this covenant, even too well. In return, when it came to the test, God had abandoned him and had made Jackson triumph, and to Adams, Jackson was the materialization of the principle of evil. Jackson was, to use Mr. Adams' own words when he was asked to attend at Harvard when the University made Jackson a Doctor of Laws, "a barbarian who could not write a sentence of grammar and hardly could spell his own name." And more than this, Jackson embodied the principle of public plunder, which Adams believed to be fatal to the hopes of posterity as well as to those of his own generation. As we can perceive now Mr. Adams had utterly mistaken the probable sequence of cause and effect. He had labored all his life to bring the democratic principle of equality into such a relation with science and education that it would yield itself into becoming, or being formed into, an efficient instrument for collective administration. But this was striving after a contradiction in human nature. Education stimulated the desire for wealth, and the desire for wealth reacted on applied science, thus making, in the language of my brother Henry, after 1830, "when the great development of physical energies began, all school teaching," that is to say all the education which Mr. Adams strove to stimulate, learn " to take for granted that man's progress in mental energy is measured by his capture of physical forces, amounting to some fifty million steam horse power from coal. . . . He cares little what becomes of all this new power, he is satisfied to know . . . that his mind has learned to control them." In short, Mr. Adams in fact stimulated an education of waste, and what he sought for was an education of conservation. But an education of conservation was contrary to the instinct of greed which dominated the democratic mind, and impelled it to insist on the pillage of the public by the private man.

And it was precisely here that Mr. Adams fell a victim to that fallacy which underlies the whole theory of modern democracy — that it is possible by education to stimulate the selfish instinct of competition, which demands that each man should strive to better himself at the cost of his neighbor, so as to coincide with the moral principle that all should labor for the common good. The one, as Mr. Adams found, meant Jackson and war, the other meant, or possibly under another order of society might be made to mean, Jesus Christ's kingdom and peace. But Mr. Adams found by sad experience that the statesman and moralist cannot combine the two.

To me this supplication of my ancestor, which was to be his requiem, is unutterably sad. The old man knew that he was dying and that he left the work, which he had hoped to do, undone. Was it through his own fault, or because God had betrayed him, — or was there no God? This much, at least he knew, on that Sunday morning: Instead of leaving his country a land of peace and freedom, as he had trusted that he might, he left her facing disunion and war. To me his words are an epitome of the lamentation of mankind through all the ages, at the fate of their efforts to ameliorate their lot on earth.

On Mr. Adams the irrevocable blow had fallen in the election of 1828, and this is how he viewed that social revolution, and how it affected him, and how it still affects us, and how it may well affect the world forevermore.

Since long before the birth of history mankind has

recognized, consciously or unconsciously, that for them the principle of evil has been embodied in the instincts of greed and avarice which are the essence of competition, and which are, perhaps, the strongest of human passions. This lust for wealth or wealth's equivalent, the primitive man personified in some malignant demon who fostered wars and pests, and who, if left to work without hindrance, would make the world a waste. Hence the origin of municipal law. For law is nothing but a series of regulations imposed on the strong for the protection of the weak, else would the weak be speedily annihilated by the sword, or enslaved by conquest.

But no code of human origin has been satisfactory because it has been the work of the strong and has consciously, for the most part, favored their interests, at the cost of the weak. Therefore none have worked justice. And consequently man has always yearned for a moral law which should reflect the thought of a supreme, benevolent being, by whose means even-handed justice should be done. Such was the vision which Mr. Adams harbored and which he explained in the letter to Mr. Edwards of Andover which I have quoted. But this was not all of the puritan's dream. Mr. Adams knew as a practical man that nothing breeds war as does want or temptation. Thus were the barbarian incursions on the

Roman Empire stimulated, and thus was projected the attack of England on Spain, in the West Indies. But these peoples were under pressure; never since the world was made, had any community been so favored as was the American by the gift by Providence of what was practically, for them, an unlimited store of wealth, which, for many generations, would raise them above the pressure of any competition which would be likely to engender war. The only serious problem for them to solve, therefore, was how to develop this gift on a collective, and not on a competitive or selfish basis.

Dominant private interests as a motor would be fatal. Mr. Adams believed when he entered the presidency that this task might be done by an honest executive, relatively easily, were he supported by an intelligent and educated civil service, who should hold their places permanently, who should be true public servants, and who should be able to devote their whole time, energy, and thought to the work. Were a single capitalistic or speculative class to get control, the interest of the whole must be sacrificed to the few and ancient injustice must prevail.

For the type of government which Mr. Adams contemplated had necessarily to be one capable of conducting a complex organism on scientific principles. The rule therefore must be rigid that public office should be a trust

G

to be won and held by merit alone. It so chanced that John McLean of Ohio had been appointed Postmaster General in 1821, a place which controlled more patronage and had more political influence than any other office under government, and McLean, being an able man and a good administrator, had raised his department to a level of efficiency never attained before. But McLean was an unscrupulous politician and an adherent of Jackson and Calhoun, and therefore bitterly hostile to Henry Clay and to the whole administration, of which Clay was recognized as being the creator. Clay, though a good practical political manager, was an honest and a loyal man, besides being a gentleman, and Clay understood the situation and remonstrated, pointing out that however improper it might be for a president to use the civil service for selfish purposes, it was worse for him to permit his adversary so to abuse it. But although Mr. Adams admitted the soundness of this reasoning in theory, he was totally incapable of reducing it to practice. He could not divest himself of the notion that in dismissing an official, he was judging his own cause, and if there were a doubt, he must decide against himself. Therefore, though finally convinced of McLean's treachery, he let him remain in office until General Jackson rewarded him by first offering him a seat in his cabinet and then making him a justice of the Supreme Court.   At length Mr. Adams conceded "that the conduct of McLean has been of deep and treacherous duplicity." Yet still he allowed him to remain.   And he did so because he could not bring himself to fight his enemy with his own weapons.   To have done so would have been in his eyes to violate his covenant with God.   Moreover, as a man, he could not have competed with Jackson for the "spoils."   Therefore the tide closed over him with hardly a ripple.

In the election of 1828 Adams was defeated by a majority of more than two to one in the electoral college, and he retired from office with what constancy he might, though he well knew that he had in vain sacrificed himself and his friends to his reliance on Providence, in spite of the entreaties of all who wished him well, especially of Mr. Clay.   Even at that early moment he saw in glaring distinctness what had happened, and what must be the result of the abandonment by God of the American people.   On the last day of the year Clay and he had a sombre interview.   "Mr. Clay spoke to me with great concern of the prospects of the country — the threats of disunion from the South, and the grasping after all the public lands, which are disclosing themselves in the Western States."

Nothing in later human experience could fit more

exactly into Henry's theory of the degradation of energy than this picture of the fall of the Adams administration of 1828, because we have so exact a standard of comparison by which to measure it. When the constitution had been adopted and the first administration organized, General Washington's personality had been so commanding that he had raised, as it were, the whole nation to his own level, by a sort of miracle of inherent strength; but after General Washington died, the democratic system of averages began its work, and the old inequality sank to a common level. By 1828, a level of degradation had been reached, and it was the level of Jackson. Therefore the fall in intelligence and intellectual energy of the democratic community, in twenty-five years, had exactly corresponded to the interval which separated George Washington intellectually, from Andrew Jackson. In short, it had been terrifying, and so Mr. Adams, who perfectly appreciated the catastrophe, felt it.

Mr. Adams, in 1832, sadly admitted to himself how he had imagined "this federative Union was to last for ages. I now disbelieve its duration for twenty years, and doubt its continuance for five." Mr. Adams' estimate of time was close, almost as close as Henry's has been in "Phase."

Alike, from Mr. Adams' point of view or from ours, the

test had been crucial. Democracy had failed to justify itself. Man alone, unaided by a supernatural power, could not resist the pressure of self-interest and of greed. He must yield to the temptation of competition. As Saint Paul said in the Epistle to the Romans, "For I delight in the law of God after the inward man:

" But I see another law in my members, warring against the law of my mind, and bringing me into captivity to the law of sin which is in my members."

And so it has always been. Competition is the law of the flesh, and in a contest between the flesh and the spirit, in the end the flesh must prevail.

"O wretched man that I am! who shall deliver me from the body of this death?"

Above this level of servitude to "the flesh," or competition, democracy could not rise. On the contrary democracy then deified competition, preaching it as the highest destiny and true duty of man. And Mr. Adams himself found to his horror that he, who had worshipped education and science, had unwittingly ministered to the demon. In that case, however innocently, he must have been guilty. He had furthered science with all his might. He did so still, even to the death. Was he to blame? On the other hand there was the alternative of admitting that there was no God, no conscious ruler of the universe, no unity, and no immortality. Better than to face this alternative were infinite and eternal self-abasement.

All this Mr. Adams had endured, and he insisted in his Diary that had he been endowed with the genius to adequately relate what he had seen and suffered during his life, he would have converted the most recalcitrant to the "law." In fact, he would have influenced no one, more than did Saint Paul. Men are not swayed by words but by impinging forces, and by suffering. Christ taught that we should love our enemies. To compete successfully the flesh decrees that we must kill them. And the flesh prevails.

CHAPTER IV

The Heritage of Henry Adams

UNLESS my memory fails me it must have been in 1884 that Mr. Scudder, who was at that time editing for Messrs. Houghton, Mifflin and Company, asked me to prepare for him a volume on Massachusetts, for the Commonwealth Series, which should be ready in two years. I told Mr. Scudder that I would do what I could, if he wished it, but that I had faint hopes of success, for I found it impossible to write to order. If I tried so to write, I always found myself to be only an amanuensis,— a clerk who held a pen, it is true, but one who wrote down the thoughts of a being over whom he had no control, and who often thought thoughts which astonished, not to say alarmed me.

Mr. Scudder declined to take me seriously, but laughingly rejoined that he would assume that risk if I would go ahead. I said no more, but went ahead for two years, and at the end of that time I brought Mr. Scudder my copy, saying to him : "My worst apprehensions have been realized. It won't do for you. I knew it would not when I began." Mr. Scudder civilly took my manuscript, read it and gave it me back, saying: "You were right. It won't do, but I shall recommend the firm to publish it all the same." And so he did, and thus I became the author of the "Emancipation of Massachusetts," which greatly scandalized all the reputable historians of Massachusetts and elsewhere, but none, I fear, more than my own brother Charles.

This, however, was only the beginning of my experience with Massachusetts theology, which the orthodox assured me I did not comprehend. For in writing that book, I had raised within me a devouring curiosity to understand, if I could, sundry problems which I have since dealt with in the preface to a subsequent volume called "The Law of Civilization and Decay," which intimately concerns Henry, for had it not been for him, that book would never have seen the light. After printing the "Emancipation," as soon as I could command the time, I began my work on my new venture and read theology backward to the schoolmen and the crusades, and then I went to Europe to try to find something on the spot. I looked at countless churches and castles and battlefields, and at last I made up my mind that I must go to Palestine. That same summer I came home and married, explaining to the woman who consented to share my fortunes, which were likely to be none of the most brilliant, as I had explained to Mr. Scudder, that I was eccentric almost to madness, and that, if she married me, she must do so on her own responsibility and at her own risk. Like Mr. Scudder, she seemed to regard this as a kind of poor joke, but, in the end, she found it serious enough. And, like Mr. Scudder, she bore the consequences of her bargain with patience, and wandered with me uncomplaining over half the earth, going in succession to England, to France, to Germany, to Algeria, to Italy, to Egypt, to Syria, to Turkey, to India, to Russia, to the West Indies, and to Mexico.

And as I wandered, and looked at the remains of the past and considered the topography of the lands I had visited, ideas came to me as wide as the poles from what I had previously supposed such ideas could be. I can see myself now as I stood one day amidst the ruins of Baalbek, and I can still feel the shock of surprise I then felt, when the conviction dawned upon me, which I have since heard denounced as a monstrous free silver invention, that the fall of Rome came about by a competition between slave and free labor and an inferiority in Roman industry. The two combined caused a contraction of the currency, and a consequent fall in prices by reason of a drain of silver to the East, and in this way brought on the panic described by Tacitus as occurring under Tiberius, which was followed by the adulteration of the denarius under Nero.

When I had thus gathered, as I thought, enough material for my immediate wants, we came home, and I established myself in my father's old house in Quincy, and I set myself to digest the chaos in my mind, but I soon found that to be a far more arduous undertaking than I had looked for, and it was more than two years before I had brought my theory into anything like a concrete form.

In the midst of my labors the panic of 1893 broke out and I found my private affairs, with those of my brothers John and Charles, seriously involved. Not knowing what else to do, I telegraphed to my brother Henry, who was spending the summer in Switzerland with Senator and Mrs. Cameron, to come to me at Quincy, as no one knew what might happen and I feared the worst, and this although Henry himself was not in the least affected by our indiscretions. And Henry, like the good fellow and the good brother he was, answered my telegram and letter in person, and stayed with me in Quincy, to my huge delight. I can see him now as I look out of my window, as he used to stroll in the garden toward sunset.

But I had something else beside my pecuniary embarrassment to talk about. I had my incomplete manuscript and Henry in my house, and I had no mind to lose what was to me such an invaluable opportunity. So one day, when we were relatively at leisure, I produced my potential book and said to Henry: "Please read this manuscript for me and tell me whether it is worth printing or whether it is quite mad. Probably there is nothing of value in it. But I want to know the fact, and you are far saner than I. All the family know it and frankly say so." And Henry, like the angel he was, took the half legible sheets and read them carefully, and then he said to me one day, "Brooks, your book is good and worth printing, but I must warn you, it will cost you dear. I know not if you have any political or other ambitions, but this will be their death blow. The gold-bugs will never forgive you. You are monkeying with a dynamo."

"Very good," said I. "That is what I want to know. I am not asking whether my book will lead to fortune, but whether it is sound history and philosophy or whether it is the dream of a maniac." "Your book is not the dream of a maniac," said he. "It is an attempt at the philosophy of history, and I am inclined to think it sound. But, I repeat, you had better not publish. You must expect no open support from me. I have no vocation for martyrdom. And you will be attacked far worse than you were attacked for the 'Emancipation.'"

"So be it," said I. "I have no ambition to compete with Daniel Webster as the jackal of the vested interests. And, as for me, I am of no earthly importance. I had rather starve and rot and keep the privilege of speaking the truth as I see it, than of holding all the offices that capital has to give from the presidency downward. What troubles me is this. I should like to have some credit for what I have done, for I have worked hard. Supposing I publish, as the world is now, no matter how I may protest or what I may say, or what evidence I may give, I shall be charged with having written a free silver squib. These gold-bugs are not historians nor do they care for truth. What they want is success no matter how it comes. They could not comprehend if they would, nor would they if they could, nor would any of the endowed universities admit, that no man could bring together such a mass of complicated evidence in the time allowed by the pressure of a political campaign. And moreover," I continued, "you must admit that history gives me no loophole for escape, supposing I tell the truth. The course of events from the crusades, and long before, leads in direct sequence to the present crisis, and I cannot avoid it or alter it. It is there. What can I do?"

"Of that, you must be the judge," said he. "I have given you fair warning. The wisest thing you can do for your own interests now or hereafter, is to hold your tongue. I shall hold mine, for I do not intend to mix in any political scrape of yours. Don't think it."

To this I rejoined: "Don't you see, Henry, how illogical you are? Here have I, for years, been preparing a book to show how strong hereditary personal characteristics are, while the world changes fast, and that a type must rise or fall according as it is adjusted to its environment. It is seldom that a single family can stay adjusted through three generations. That is a demonstrable fact. It is now full four generations since John Adams wrote the constitution of Massachusetts. It is time that we perished. The world is tired of us. We have only survived because our ancestors lived in times of revolution. Both our grandfather and our great grandfather were obnoxious to the gold-bugs of their time. I should hardly be true bred, were I loved by those of mine. You remember what John Quincy Adams wrote to his father when he remonstrated with him, as you remonstrate with me. 'I have heard of a highway robber who, upon going to the scaffold was asked, why he had not been deterred from leading such a life, by fear of the halter.' He answered: 'It is only one disease that we are more subject to than others.' Elsewhere he added philosophically, 'Man can only be what God and nature made him.'

And so John Quincy Adams went on to meet his fate. You know you think that fate tragic. And so I must take my chances. They won't be brilliant, of that be sure." "If that is your view," said he, "go on and take your fate, and God be with you, only I have no taste that way. My connections lie elsewhere. But my advice to you is that if you are resolved to publish, as I think you are justified in doing, choose rather a publisher in London than here. In London there is a possibility that they may take you seriously. Here certainly they will not. Passions are running too strong, and the gold-bugs have too much at stake."

If I live forever, I shall never forget that summer. Henry and I sat in the hot August evenings and talked endlessly of the panic and of our hopes and fears, and of my historical and economic theories, and so the season wore away amidst an excitement verging on revolution. Henry, of course, was much less keenly personally interested than I, but as he very frankly says in his "Education," his instincts led toward silver. My historical studies led the same way, as well as my private situation, as one of the debtor class.

A long series of investigations comprising many, many centuries, had forced me to the conclusion that humanity competes in various ways, by war, for example, in which case slavery is apt to follow defeat, and by usury, which takes the form of a struggle between debtor and creditor, when slavery may also be the fate of the vanquished. All of which I have stated at length in the preface to "Civilization and Decay," and which I only allude to here, because it serves to illuminate the working of Henry's mind, and shows how he came to "Phase." And, practically, my inference was this in 1893 : Mostly men work unconsciously, and perform an act, before they can explain why; often centuries before. Throughout the ages it had been the favorite device of the creditor class first to work a contraction of the currency, which bankrupted the debtors, and then to cause an inflation which created a rise when they sold the property which they had impounded. The question with me was, how fully was I justified in applying these admitted facts of history to the crisis of 1893. Beginning with the panic at Rome under Tiberius, I had a long list of precedents stretching through the crusades to the present time. And the common way for many centuries, in which an advance after a depression had been secured, was by an adulteration or debasement of the currency, and at a later day by an issue of paper. But the men who had usually conducted such vast movements had to be supremely adapted to the business.

We then here called them "gold-bugs." The question between Henry and me, as I then stated it, was, assuming the general law of the past to hold, whether our family could keep solvent until relief came, or whether we should go under like the Roman peasants or like the British yeomen. Henry thought, or was inclined to think, that we should be crushed. I thought that, with good luck, courage, economy, and patience, we should be able to hold on until relief in some form came, and crawl in with the bankers on the rise. Which, in fact, we subsequently did, but the process stimulated thought. And it was then, as Henry has pointed out in his "Education," that his great effort at thought began.

The immediate effect of this stimulant to Henry, of which I presently became aware, was in the following winter when he wrote as a "communication" to the "American Historical Association" of which he was then president, the first of the following documents, which is also the first of his contributions to scientific history, and I think one of the ablest. Afterward he explained to me that he had written it as a sort of preface or introduction to my proposed book, which I was then making ready to print during the following spring. "For," said he, "without something of the sort, one of two things will happen to you. Either you will be altogether ignored by the old expedient of the 'conspiracy of silence,' or you will be attacked with fury." "For," he continued, "the teaching profession is, like the church and the bankers, a vested interest. And the historians will fall on any one who threatens their stock in trade quite as virulently as do the bankers on the silver men. So you may judge. Certainly, if you succeed, history can no longer be taught in the old way." No one before or since has stated the ruthlessness of scientific history more pungently and at the same time delicately than has Henry in this paper. He has shown how scientific history can support no party and no interest. It must be a summary of a complex of conflicting forces. But my opinion is that this essay went over the heads of his audience by about a generation. It would have more chance of being appreciated now. Then it was set down as an eccentricity without practical application. And so it was forgotten.

The next summer I passed at Quincy in putting "Civilization and Decay" through the press, a process which Henry watched with interest. Before it appeared here in America, I had sailed for India and I saw Henry no more for a year. But while waiting in Rome for the Bombay ship, I received from him the following letter, which even then seemed to me a criticism of surpassing

H

interest, and which, in the light of the past, seems to me now to excel anything which was produced at anywhere near that time.

DEAR BROOKS:

I write you a line merely to say that I hope to go south next week, and you may not hear from me again while you are in India. As far as I can see, the scrimmage is over. The nations, after a display of dreadful bad manners, are settling down, afraid to fight. The gold-bugs have resumed their sway, with their nerves a good deal shaken, but their tempers or their sense unimproved.

Cleveland and Olney have relapsed into their normal hog-like attitudes of indifference, and Congress is disorganized, stupid and childlike as ever. Once more we are under the whip of the bankers. Even on Cuba, where popular feeling was far stronger than on Venezuela, we are beaten and hopeless. . . .

My turn will come next, and I am all ready and glad to get through it. The last six weeks have given me much to think about. Were we on the edge of a new and last great centralization, or of a first great movement of disintegration? There are facts on both sides; but my conclusion rather is — and this is what satiates my instinct for life — that our so-called civilization has shown its movement, even at the centre, arrested. It has failed to concentrate further. Its next effort may succeed, but it is more likely to be one of disintegration, with Russia for the eccentric on one side and America on the other. . . .

In either case, the next great conclusive movement is likely to take at least one full generation. If, as I think, we move much faster than the Romans, we have more ground to cover, and fewer outside enemies to fear. As I read the elder Pliny, I am struck by the astonishing parity between him and you. He came about a hundred years after the military age ended, and the police age began. You write just eighty years after the same epoch. Pliny died in the year 79. Three hundred years afterwards Ammianus Marcellinus closed his history with the death of Valens and the practical overthrow of Roman civilization, in 378. Allowing for our more rapid movement we ought still to have more than two hundred years of futile and stupid stagnation. I find twenty too much for me.

The process of turning a machine like ours round a corner will be dangerous in proportion to its sharpness, but neither its dangers, nor its successes, nor its failures seem to me now to be worth living to see. Nothing can come of it that is worth living for; nothing so interesting as we have already seen; and nothing better to say. I understand that your book has been exhausted in New York for some time, and that Macmillan is waiting for more copies. The longer we can keep it working under ground the better. If it once gets notorious, as it well may, under the blessed pressure of the gold standard which turns even defeats into victories for us, I want you to print it in a cheap form for popular reading. It is, as I have always told you, the Bible of Anarchy. God knows what side in our politics it would help, for it cuts all equally, but it might help man to know himself and hark back to God. For after all man knows mighty little, and may some day learn enough of his own ignorance to fall down again and pray. Not that I care. Only, if such is God's will, and Fate and Evolution — let there be God!

Anyway I have been correcting and annotating a copy in case you want my suggestions for your next edition. . . . But just now the gold-bugs have got their loans and foreign policy, and the next presidency safe, as far as I can see, and I shall go fishing.

I go with the easier temper because I see that what I want is really their right game, and what they get is merely a prolongation of the anarchy now prevailing. Not one question has been settled. All the old, and several new ones, are as active as ever, and more virulent. Our revolt has been a slave insurrection, but we have given our masters a mauvais quart d'heure, and cost them a very pretty sum of hard money. And above all, I have had my fun.

Ever yours,

Henry was as good as his word. He did annotate a copy of the London edition which I now have before me, and which served to help me in the preparation of the Macmillan edition which appeared the next year, but he did more than this. He conceived the idea that I should publish a French translation, and for that purpose he annotated a copy of the Macmillan edition, elaborately, and never rested until I went to Paris and, near him, superintended the translation and publication of an edition in 1899, which I tried to make as exhaustive and as exact as possible. But even this did not satisfy him. He complained to me that my preface was imperfect and that it should be more scientific. "Don't you see,

Brooks," he would say to me again and again, as he sat in my house in Paris, "that you, with your lawyer's method, only state sequences of fact, and explain no causes? Granting that your sequences are correct, and I believe they are, and that your law is sound, which I am willing to suppose, you do not tell us why man has been a failure, and could be nothing but a failure. You only show that he has failed.

"To leave human development where you do is hardly satisfactory nor is it surely scientific history. If there be a God and a consequent unity, man should confess him. Then indeed he may have a chance of steady advancement toward perfection. But, if there be no unity and on the contrary only multiplicity, he can only develop into that chaos of which he forms a part. Therefore," he would say, "you should write a scientific summary."

But such a task was beyond me. Therefore, I declined Henry's suggestion to join him in Paris and work at the scheme which he proposed, and went back to my old life in America. From that time Henry lost interest in my further publications, though he continued faithfully to read them, but always with the same complaint, "that I got nowhere." On the other hand he took up "scientific history" himself, and soon became immersed in it. Nor could it have been otherwise with a man of his energy of mind. The twelfth and thirteenth centuries are the most fascinating portions of the life of the modern world and Henry luxuriated in them. The result may be read in "Mont St. Michel and Chartres," and while I have permitted myself to criticise some aspects of that book, I conceive it to be, on the whole, by far the greatest attempt at a historical generalization that exists in any language.

Meanwhile he was reading pure science with all the avidity of John Quincy Adams when he prepared his "Weights and Measures," and when I visited Washington, as I did each winter, I went straight to Henry's house and we plunged into a talk which was apt to last till near morning. That was in the beginning, but as time elapsed I noticed a change come over him, which troubled me. His nerves seemed to lose their firmness. He complained that "he could not be agitated," and that if we talked late, he could not sleep. And so he came rather to shun me, seeming to prefer women's society, in which he could be amused and tranquillized. Notwithstanding this slight estrangement, I well knew that his scientific studies went on, and I awaited with anxiety the result. For a scientific theory is worthless unless applied to facts, and although I was delighted with "Mont St. Michel and Chartres," I felt it to be but one third of his task were he to be understood. Another volume ought to take him to the Reformation, and a third to our own day, I hoped to our grandfather, on whom we had labored together and on whom I had failed, because probably, I did not understand the scientific side of my subject. If any one could succeed with him, it would be Henry.

But Henry, after "Mont St. Michel," drifted off into his "Education," in which, as I warned him to weariness, I feared that he had attempted too much. I told him that he had tried to mix science with society and that the public would never understand his scientific theory. He insisted that he could make his theory plain. And then, before he had time to go further, he had his illness, and, to my eternal regret, he will never now go on to fill the gap which he has left. And, for that reason, I am making this meagre effort.

Regarded philosophically, Henry's life is, in effect, a continuation of his grandfather's; he is part of a large intellectual movement and his life is, to a certain degree, mixed with my own. I try, as well as I can, to put them all together. My grandfather speaks for himself. My books, at best, are but a poor epitome of what would have been Henry's monumental exposition to sustain and prove his philosophy, but I have no better to offer.

I have now ended my review of the facts which, taken in the connection with those related in Henry's Autobiography, explain, as I hope, the nature of the environment which, at a given moment, produced the phenomenon of Henry's mind in a typical New England family like that of my father. But in order that this intellectual inheritance as a sequence may be incisive, I apprehend that I should at the close of my story present a summary, since, as I have elsewhere pointed out, generalizations of this description resemble the fragments of a mutilated inscription which cannot be read until the scattered stones have been set in a predetermined order. In this case the work is the easier because we are concerned with the rise and progress of American democracy, and the beginning of the movement as well as the form it took and the standard which must serve as the measure of its advance or recession in intellectual power, is to be computed according to the personality of George Washington, who, without doubt, stands at the apex of democratic civilization.

Thus, the model and the standard of John Quincy Adams was George Washington, and to him it was from the very outset clear that, if the democratic social system were capable of progression upward to a level at which it could hope to ameliorate the lot of men on earth, it must tend, at least, to produce an average which, if it did not attain to the eminent ability of the first President, might at least be capable of understanding and appreciating his moral altitude.

In every civilization there are, as Saint Paul pointed out, two principles in conflict, — the law, or the moral principle, and the flesh, or the evil principle; and the flesh is, in a general way, incarnated in the principle of competition, which, rooted in the passions of greed, avarice, and cruelty, is apt to prevail to an unendurable degree unless restrained by law. And it is to regulate and restrain competition that human laws have been and are still devised. Washington had already formulated in his mind, even before he first assumed the presidency, an elaborate theory of how a diffused community might be built up into a consolidated and efficient unity; and, stated concisely, his theory amounted to this, comprising both material and intellectual concentration. The first requisite was to suppress competition among the parts, that is, to keep order; and, to keep order, there must be a centre of energy whose will must dominate. Governments, according to Washington, are not accidents, they are growths, and growths which may be consciously fostered and stimulated, or smothered, according as more or less intelligence is generated in the collective brain. The material energy is collected at the heart of the organism, which is the central market or seat of exchanges, and which can only be successfully developed at the point of convergence of the main highways or arteries of commerce, which nourish the provinces. Washington judged that, in the example before him, the natural highways or paths of least resistance were the rivers, which, with their tributaries, drained the Mississippi Valley, and which, by a canal, might be connected with the Potomac and there, at a point where bulk had to be broken, at their junction with ocean navigation, might generate a capital of the first magnitude. The point he selected was the site of the present city of Washington, whose influence, incidentally, should convert Virginia because of her resources in iron and coal into an industrial community, and thus into a free state. But Washington's conception of national life and national progression did not stop here. He felt strongly that the national intelligence must keep pace with the national accumulation of wealth, and to this end a national system of education should be crowned by a national university, which should be the chief instrument for the stimulation of thought. Without such an instrument he doubted if the standard of democratic intelligence could be made to rise rather than to fall.

As I have already insisted, perhaps to satiety, this grandiose conception of Washington broke down for several reasons. In the first place, lacking the stimulus of his mind, the community, as a whole, could not be brought to the point of building its own highways, but left their location and construction to private competition. Thus the line of the Ohio and the Potomac, instead of becoming the bond which should bind North and South together, became the line of cleavage; and the cotton gin, by causing the growth of slaves to become, for the moment, more profitable than the development of its iron and coal, turned Virginia into a slave stock-farm, thereby making the Civil War inevitable.

Mr. Adams sought to vitalize Washington's policy during his administration, and failed. Defeated in 1828, no sooner was the election a thing of the past than he fell to measuring, to satisfy his own mind, the space through which democracy had fallen during his own lifetime, and he found the degradation appalling. In 1832 Congress asked John A. Washington to permit the body of General Washington to be removed from Mount Vernon and entombed under the Capitol. Washington declined. Thereupon Mr. Adams made this comment: "I did wish that this resolution might have been carried into execution, but this wish was connected with an imagination that this federative Union was to last for ages. I now disbelieve its duration for twenty years, and doubt its continuance for five." In fact, the Union was dissolved by secession in 1861, — precisely twenty-nine years, — which is a contraction of span representing a fall of potential, as Henry would call it, from infinity to zero. And the cause of this shrinkage is clear. The original union and the original administrative system of the government was, as far as so complex an organism might be, the product of Washington's single mind and of his commanding personality. Hardly had Washington gone to his grave when the levelling work of the system of averages, on which democracy rests, began. And it worked in all its parts with freedom and success. Domestic competition could hardly have been more thorough and consistent. And the result was war and disunion. Nor has peace on a democratic basis ever been established in the South since. Another generation passed and Mr. Adams' grandson, in 1870, sat in the gallery of Congress and listened to the announcement of Grant's cabinet. He has recorded his impressions. He blushed for himself because he had dreamed it to be possible that a democratic republic could develop the intellectual energy to raise itself to that advanced level of intelligence which had been accepted as a moral certainty by Washington, his own grandfather, and most of his grandfather's contemporaries in the eighteenth century, and whose dreams and ideas he had, as he describes, unconsciously inherited. He understood at length, as his ancestor had learned, that mankind does not advance by his own unaided efforts, and competition, toward perfection. He does not automatically realize unity or even progress. On the contrary, he reflects the diversity of nature. It is the contrast between the ideal of the kingdom of heaven, peace and obedience; and the diversity of competition, or, in other words, of war. Democracy is an infinite mass of conflicting minds and of conflicting interests which, by the persistent action of such a solvent as the modern or competitive industrial system, becomes resolved into what is, in substance, a vapor, which loses in collective intellectual energy in proportion to the perfection of its expansion.

Another twenty-five years were to elapse, and the theory was advanced that the economic centre of the world determined the social equilibrium, and that this international centre of exchanges was an ambulatory spot on the earth's surface which seldom remained fixed for any considerable period of time, but which vibrated back and forth according as discoveries in applied science and geography changed avenues of communication, and caused trade routes to reconverge. Thus Babylon had given way to Rome, Rome to Constantinople, Constantinople to Venice, Venice to Antwerp, and finally, about 1810, London became the undisputed capital of the world. Each migration represented a change in equilibrium, and, therefore, caused a social convulsion. At the outset this theory was derided. Such theories always are. But toward the period of the Boer War it was suggested that the supremacy of London appeared to be vacillating, and then it was taken more seriously. Indeed, by that time, the symptoms had become pretty convincing. They had first been noticed as far back as the panic of 1890 in London, which ruined the Barings. That local panic was followed by a contraction which induced the panic of 1893 at home, with which I have already dealt, and by 1900 there were symptoms of instability which suggested that the economic capital of civilization was already tending to shift toward America. The relative production of pig iron, for example, was significant. Nor were these the most alarming phenomena. England betrayed feebleness in the face of the attack of German competition, which had been growing fiercer ever since the consolidation of Germany after the War of 1870. But if these facts were true, and they could not be seriously denied, it was evident, on inspection, that civilization stood poised on the brink of a portentous crisis. For if the centre of exchanges, which had been stationary in London ever since Waterloo, should migrate either east

or west, — either to New York or to Berlin, — a conflict
must ensue which would shake the whole world, since
all the world had become a part of an organic whole,
by reason of the intense stimulation of movement. No
one, however, suspected that the catastrophe was imminent. I suggested its date myself as probably about
1930, but no one took me seriously. It actually came in
1914. Alone Henry, in "Phase," which he sent me two
years before the war broke out, in 1912, elaborated a
mathematical theory by which he predicted the catastrophe, before the event. Even I, then, thought he was
exaggerating. I earnestly refer the reader, who may be
interested, to "Phase."

As Henry neared the end of his application of the
development of the thirteenth century according to
scientific historical theory, in "Mont St. Michel and
Chartres," he turned more and more toward his next step
in the "Reformation," on which he constantly talked
with me. He found the "Reformation" most antago-
nistic, chiefly, I think, because of the Puritan attack on
women; for it was during the Reformation that the
Virgin was dethroned and, according to his theory, I
take it, that the degradation of woman began. For it
is precisely here that I wish to point out a legal and
philosophical distinction — one which hinges, as Henry

explains in the "Letter to Teachers," on the distinction between reason and instinct. Now as a lawyer and as a historian, I insist that society, as an organism, has little or no interest in woman's reason, but its very existence is bound up in her instincts. Intellectually, woman's reason has been a matter of indifference to men. As an intellectual competitor she has never been formidable; but maternity is a monopoly. It is the *passionate* instinct which is the cause and the effect of maternity, and which enables women to serve their great purpose as the cement of society. As an intellectual being, as the modern feminist would make her, she has only the importance of a degraded boy, though she is far more dangerous to society than such a boy would be, who would be relatively harmless.

It was, perhaps, during discussions such as these, that Henry grew curious to test the thought of the scientific world, and accordingly he wrote toward 1910 his "Letter to Teachers," which I then thought, and think even more strongly now than then, to have been the ablest exposition of the scientific theory of the degradation of energy and of the issue between intellect and instinct which has ever been made. If, as I have good reason to infer, the reception which this little book met with among the class to whom it was sent, was a disappointment to

Henry, in so far as it left them indifferent, it had at least
a very great effect on me. I found, among other things,
that if Henry had written this essay as a commentary
upon his ancestor's life and fortunes, it could not have
been more absolutely to the point, and this pleased me
the more and was to me the more remarkable and convincing, as I do not imagine that Henry had, when he
wrote it, John Quincy Adams at all in mind as a text
for his discourse. I have only now to beg such of my
readers as may be interested in these questions to read
my account of my ancestor's misfortunes, in his dealing
with democracy, and then turn to Henry's essay especially where, as for example on page 156, he goes into
the question of the "degradation of energies"; or what
he has to say on the relation of instinct to reason, when
it comes to a consideration of the feminine question, on
page 203. "The mere act of reproduction, which seems
to have been the most absorbing and passionate purpose
of primitive instinct, concerns history not at all," page 206.
Certainly it does not concern the modern feminist, who
repudiates such an instinct as unworthy of a civilized
and educated modern woman, and by so doing announces
herself as incapable of performing the only function in
modern society which has the least vital importance to
mankind. I come now to the consideration of "Phase,"

I

which is an attempt by means of a mathematical formula, based on the facts of past events, to determine the date at which social revolutions may occur ; and to me this effort of Henry's is of intense, I may say of painful, interest. But it is also a sphere of his work in which I feel least competent to accompany him. I am inclined in "Phase" to surrender my judgment completely to his. This I say at once frankly. Some dozen years or more before "Phase" was produced the theory was advanced by me and was more or less accepted by Henry in the approval which he gave in general to "Civilization and Decay."

Henry, in "Phase," reached a conclusion which even I thought exaggerated. He in 1912 named the year 1917 as the date at which a probably revolutionary acceleration of thought would take place, and in fact in that year America was drawn into the war by the resistless attraction of the British economic system, and to-day Great Britain and America, like the parts of some gigantic saurian which has been severed in a prehistoric contest, seem half unconsciously to be trying to unite in an economic organism, perhaps to be controlled by a syndicate of bankers who will direct the movements of the putative governments of this enormous aggregation of vested interests independent of the popular will.

And this brings me to the somewhat alarming task of considering Henry's forecast in "Phase," of the world's possible future. For though it is generally conceded that the outlook for civilization is murky, Henry's calculation suggests that its catastrophe may be actually at hand.

Assuming that we are still in the mechanical phase, and using the same formula which he used in his estimate touching the year 1917, Henry finds that we may probably enter the "ethereal phase" in 1921, or in somewhere about two years from the present time, when thought will reach the limit of its possibilities. How such an age would express itself must be to most of us problematical, since, according to Henry, only a few highly trained and gifted men will then be able to understand each other; but attempting to translate such hypothetical thought into ordinary legal or political terms, the more we reflect upon what we see going on about us, the less unreasonable such a limit of time becomes. Supposing thought to indeed reach its limit, and action to correspond to the intensity of the acceleration of thought, as it always hitherto has done, we reach a social condition which is already to a certain degree indicated.

For some years past many symptoms seem not obscurely to indicate that we tend to sink into that chaos of democratic mediocrity which Henry likens to the ocean, where waters which have fallen to sea level are engulfed, and can no more do useful work. In such an ocean tempests are generated by the operations of usurers, and such tempests are apt to be stilled by massacres, such as have become to us familiar of late, in countries like Armenia.

In view of what has occurred within these four or five years, such a forecast for 1921 now would be less astonishing than would a forecast of what we now behold have been, had it been made in 1912. Viewed impartially, we present the aspect of a society in extremely unstable equilibrium, which is being attacked on every hand by potent forces from without, and which is yet being preyed on from within by a destructive tumor.

It is only needful to glance, for a single instant, at the imbecility which democracy presented at Paris in its efforts to make a peace with Germany, to become conscious of the external pressure. Recently, in New York, Mr. Gary in a speech admitted that the war now closing had been an effect of competition. This fact, which has been patent from the outset to every observant mind, was at first hotly, not to say angrily, denied by the banking fraternity, lest they should be held responsible therefor, and thereby restrained in their action. Since Mr. Gary's speech, however, the fact of its having been an economic war may, probably, be assumed to be admitted. But an economic war is the fiercest and most pitiless of all wars, since to make a lasting peace in competition implies either the extermination or enslavement of the vanquished. If the vanquished is to be conciliated, that is to say, to be restored to a position in which he can act as a freeman, he must be granted rights which will enable him to compete on equal terms with the victors, and the old conditions will be automatically revived. That is to say there must be a still more bitter struggle within a generation, — at furthest.

Now this dilemma is not easy to solve. To exterminate ninety millions of Germans would be a difficult task, even for a conqueror like Jenghiz Khan, or as stern a Roman as Cato. With the modern democratic sentiment, it probably could not be done. Enslavement would be little, if any, better. In the first place, to enslave so large a part of humanity is very expensive because of the cost of maintaining an adequate guard, and secondly, slavery has been found, ever since the days of Rome, to decisively degrade the masters. Not that the present standard of democratic intelligence needs or could well withstand much degrading. It is only necessary to compare the personnel of the present commissioners at Paris with that of the Congress of Vienna after Waterloo to be assured of the movement. Nor was the Congress of Vienna either a wonderfully intelligent or successful body. Still, they shone with brilliancy in comparison with what we now have. Or take, as an illustration of the same phenomenon, the commissioners who were sent by Mr. Madison to Ghent to negotiate the peace with England in 1814, and they stand in relation to the present American delegation at Paris in pretty much the same position in which General Washington's cabinet stood to the cabinet of Jackson. It is a subject for meditation.

The upshot has been that, because of this incapacity, the bankers have apparently found it necessary to take the settlement of a peace out of the hands of the nominal political authorities and come to some agreement among themselves. What that agreement is we do not know, and perhaps may never know, save as events discover it in the future, but of this we may be certain: it will be an arrangement which will conduce to the further dominance of the great moneyed interests.

And yet, serious as this situation may appear to be in the light of the present unstable social equilibrium, it is naught beside the terrors which threaten our society, as at present organized, by the unsexing of women. Since the great industrial capitalistic movement began throughout the modern world toward 1830, the modern feminist has sought to put the woman upon a basis of legal equality at which she would be enabled, as it was thought, to become the economic competitor of man. At length, after nearly a century, and as one of the effects of the recent war, she seems to have succeeded in her ambition. So far as possible the great sexual instinct has been weakened or suppressed. So far as possible it is now ignored systematically in our education. Woman is ashamed of her sex and imitates the man. And the results are manifest enough to alarm the most optimistic and confiding. The effect has been to turn enormous numbers of women into the ranks of the lower paid classes of labor, but far worse, in substance, to destroy the influence of woman in modern civilization, save in so far as her enfranchisement tends to degrade the democratic level of intelligence. The woman, as the cement of society, the head of the family, and the centre of cohesion, has, for all intents and purposes, ceased to exist. She has become a wandering isolated unit, rather a dispersive than a collective force.

Already the working of the poison is apparent in our system of law, and it is appalling. The family principle has decayed until, as a legal conception, it has ceased to exist. The father has no authority, the wife is absolutely independent and so are the children, save so far as the state exerts a modified control, as in the matter of education. The graduated tax seeks to equalize the earning power of the individual, and the inheritance tax confiscates accumulations to the state. The advanced feminist claims for the woman the right to develop herself according to her own will. She may decline to bear children, or, if she consents, she is to bear them to whom she may choose. Such conditions, if carried out logically, must create chaos. If so, the state must regulate such matters, and the woman must be required to serve the state by bearing children as the man serves the state in the army. The state must assume the education and cost of children, when so born, and must subsequently employ them at an average wage, all thus being put on an equality. Such is the manifest direction in which the efforts of our advanced feminists tend.

It may be very confidently assumed, however, that such efforts will only result in the enslavement of the weaker or the poorer class. The rich and fortunate usurer will always enjoy exemption from all regulations which inconvenience him, even as they do now throughout the world. We have seen the working of the democratic system during the recent war. The bankers, as a class, stayed at home, and the management of all business, and, above all the fixing of prices, fell automatically into the hands of those who were the strongest. As John Quincy

Adams discovered in 1828, democracy would not permit the ablest staff of officials, to be chosen by him, to administer the public trust. Democracy, on the contrary, has insisted on degrading the public service to a common level of incapacity, thereby throwing the management of all difficult public problems, such as the use of railroads and canals, into private hands, in order that they might escape ruin, and thence has come the predicament in which we, in particular, and the world at large, now stand.

The democratic principle of public conduct has always been "that to the victor belongs the spoil," and public property has been administered accordingly. It is the system of averages or of levelling downward. We see it in the trade union. The wage is fixed according to the capacity of the feeblest workman, precisely as the pace of the regiment is fixed by the walk of the slowest horse. But under nature's system of competition the opposite tendency prevails, and prevails to a terrible excess, even to the excess of war. And social war, or massacre, would seem to be the natural ending of the democratic philosophy. Viewed thus, Henry's estimate of time seems not to be beyond the limit of probability, but whether right or wrong, in point of time, the ultimate conclusion seems to be, sooner or later, humanly speaking, a certainty.

Lastly, I have one word more touching that profoundest of problems, — Is this universe purposeful or chaotic, particularly as viewed in the light of astronomy?

Mr. Adams always loved and promoted astronomy, for, as a young man, he doubted not that he saw therein the working and the purpose of the divine mind. As he aged, doubts gathered, and I have quoted his diary, X, 39, to show whither his mind tended at seventy-one. Had he lived, he might well have reached the ground taken by his grandson in "Phase," who used the comet as the emblem of chaos. ("Phase," p. 300, et seq.) But Mr. Adams always adored order and loathed the very idea of chaos. Yet he died for astronomy, the science of chaos. Such is human effort and prescience.[1]

[1] If the reader is interested in scientific chaos, I refer him to Simon Newcomb's "Astronomy for Students," Second Edition, Chapter VII, Cosmogony, page 492, et seq.

THE TENDENCY OF HISTORY

1894

THE TENDENCY OF HISTORY [1]

GUADA'-C-JARA, December 12, 1894.

DEAR SIR: I regret extremely that constant absence has prevented me from attending the meetings of the Historical Association. On the date which your letter mentions as that of its first decennial I shall not be within reach. I have to ask you to offer my apology to the members, and the assurance that at that moment I am believed to be somewhere beyond the Isthmus of Panama. Perhaps this absence runs in some of the mysterious ways of nature's law, for you will not forget that when you did me the honor to make me your president I was still farther away — in Tahiti or Fiji, I believe — and never even had an opportunity to thank you. Evidently I am fitted only to be an absent president, and you will pardon a defect which is clearly not official, but a condition of the man.

I regret this fault the more because I would have liked to be of service, and perhaps there is service that might be usefully performed. Even the effort to hold together the persons interested in history is worth making. That we should ever act on public opinion with the weight of one compact and one energetic conviction is hardly to be expected, but that one day or another we shall be compelled to act individually or in groups I cannot doubt. With more anxiety than confidence, I should have liked

[1] A communication to the American Historical Association, as President of the Association.

125

to do something, however trifling, to hold the association together and unite it on some common ground, with a full understanding of the course which history seems destined to take and with a good-natured willingness to accept or reject the result, but in any case not to quarrel over it.

No one who has watched the course of history during the last generation can have felt doubt of its tendency. Those of us who read Buckle's first volume when it appeared in 1857, and almost immediately afterwards, in 1859, read the Origin of Species and felt the violent impulse which Darwin gave to the study of natural laws, never doubted that historians would follow until they had exhausted every possible hypothesis to create a science of history. Year after year passed, and little progress has been made. Perhaps the mass of students are more skeptical now than they were thirty years ago of the possibility that such a science can be created. Yet almost every successful historian has been busy with it, adding here a new analysis, a new generalization there; a clear and definite connection where before the rupture of idea was absolute; and, above all, extending the field of study until it shall include all races, all countries, and all times. Like other branches of science, history is now encumbered and hampered by its own mass, but its tendency is always the same, and cannot be other than what it is. That the effort to make history a science may fail is possible, and perhaps probable; but that it should cease, unless for reasons that would cause all science to cease, is not within the range of experience. Historians will not, and even if they would they can not, abandon the attempt. Science itself would admit its own failure if it admitted that man, the most important of all its subjects, could not be brought within its range.

You may be sure that four out of five serious students of history who are living to-day have, in the course of their work, felt that they stood on the brink of a great generalization that would reduce all history under a law as clear as the laws which govern the material world. As the great writers of our time have touched one by one the separate fragments of admitted law by which society betrays its character as a subject for science, not one of them can have failed to feel an instant's hope that he might find the secret which would transform these odds and ends of philosophy into one self-evident, harmonious, and complete system. He has seemed to have it, as the Spanish say, in his inkstand. Scores of times he must have dropped his pen to think how one short step, one sudden inspiration, would show all human knowledge; how, in these thickset forests of history, one corner turned, one faint trail struck, would bring him on the highroad of science. Every professor who has tried to teach the doubtful facts which we now call history must have felt that sooner or later he or another would put order in the chaos and bring light into darkness. Not so much genius or favor was needed as patience and good luck. The law was certainly there, and as certainly was in places actually visible, to be touched and handled, as though it were a law of chemistry or physics. No teacher with a spark of imagination or with an idea of scientific method can have helped dreaming of the immortality that would be achieved by the man who should successfully apply Darwin's method to the facts of human history.

Those of us who have had occasion to keep abreast of the rapid progress which has been made in history during the last fifty years must be convinced that the same rate of progress during another half century would necessarily raise history to the rank of a science. Our only doubt is whether the same rate can possibly be maintained. If not, our situation is simple. In that case, we shall remain more or less where we are. But we have reached a point where we ought to face the possibility of a great and perhaps a sudden change in the importance of our profession. We cannot help asking ourselves what would happen if some new Darwin were to demonstrate the laws of historical evolution.

I admit that the mere idea of such an event fills my mind with anxiety. When I remember the astonishing influence exerted by a mere theorist like Rousseau; by a reasoner like Adam Smith; by a philosopher, beyond contact with material interests, like Darwin, I cannot imagine the limits of the shock that might follow the establishment of a fixed science of history. Hitherto our profession has been encouraged, or, at all events, tolerated by governments and by society as an amusing or instructive and, at any rate, a safe and harmless branch of inquiry. But what will be the attitude of government or of society toward any conceivable science of history? We know what followed Rousseau; what industrial and political struggles have resulted from the teachings of Adam Smith; what a revolution and what vehement opposition has been and still is caused by the ideas of Darwin. Can we imagine any science of history that would not be vastly more violent in its effects than the dissensions roused by any one or by all three of these great men?

I ask myself, What shape can be given to any science of history that will not shake to its foundations some prodigious interest? The world is made up of a few immense forces, each with an organization that corresponds with its strength. The church stands first; and at the outset we must assume that the church will not and cannot accept any science of history, because science, by its definition, must exclude the idea of a personal and active providence. The state stands next; and the hostility of the state would be assured toward any system or science that might not strengthen its arm. Property is growing more and more timid and looks with extreme jealousy on any new idea that may weaken vested rights. Labor is growing more and more self-confident and looks with contempt on all theories that do not support its own. Yet we cannot conceive of a science of history that would not, directly or indirectly, affect all these vast social forces.

Any science assumes a necessary sequence of cause and effect, a force resulting in motion which cannot be other than what it is. Any science of history must be absolute, like other sciences, and must fix with mathematical certainty the path which human society has got to follow. That path can hardly lead toward the interests of all the great social organizations. We cannot conceive that it should help at the same time the church and the state, property and communism, capital and poverty, science and religion, trade and art. Whatever may be its orbit, it must, at least for a time, point away from some of these forces toward others which are regarded as hostile. Conceivably, it might lead off in eccentric lines away from them all, but by no power of our imagination can we conceive that it should lead toward them all.

Although I distrust my own judgment and look earnestly for guidance to those who are younger than I and closer to the movement of the time, I cannot be wholly wrong in thinking that a change has come over the tendency of

K

liberal thought since the middle of the century. Darwin led an intellectual revival much more hopeful than any movement that can now be seen in Europe, except among the socialists. Had history been converted into a science at that time it would perhaps have taken the form of cheerful optimism which gave to Darwin's conclusions the charm of a possible human perfectibility. Of late years the tone of European thought has been distinctly despondent among the classes which were formerly most hopeful. If a science of history were established to-day on the lines of its recent development I greatly fear it would take its tone from the pessimism of Paris, Berlin, London, and St. Petersburg, unless it brought into sight some new and hitherto unsuspected path for civilization to pursue.

If it pointed to a socialistic triumph it would place us in an attitude of hostility toward existing institutions. Even supposing that our universities would permit their professors in this country to announce the scientific certainty of communistic triumphs, could Europe be equally liberal? Would property, on which the universities depend, allow such freedom of instruction? Would the state suffer its foundation to be destroyed? Would society as now constituted tolerate the open assertion of a necessity which should affirm its approaching overthrow?

If, on the other hand, the new science required us to announce that the present evils of the world — its huge armaments, its vast accumulations of capital, its advancing materialism, and declining arts — were to be continued, exaggerated, over another thousand years, no one would listen to us with satisfaction. Society would shut its eyes and ears. If we proved the certainty of our results we should prove it without a sympathetic audience and without good effect. No one except artists and socialists would listen, and the conviction which we should produce on them could lead only to despair and attempts at anarchy in art, in thought, and in society.

If, finally, the science should prove that society must at a given time revert to the church and recover its old foundation of absolute faith in a personal providence and a revealed religion, it commits suicide.

In whatever direction we look we can see no possibility of converting history into a science without bringing it into hostility toward one or more of the most powerful organizations of the era. If the world is to continue moving toward the point which it has so energetically pursued during the last fifty years, it will destroy the hopes of the vast organizations of labor. If it is to change its course and become communistic, it places us in direct hostility to the entire fabric of our social and political system. If it goes on, we must preach despair. If it goes back, it must deny and repudiate science. If it goes forward, round a circle which leads through communism, we must declare ourselves hostile to the property that pays us and the institutions we are bound in duty to support.

A science cannot be played with. If an hypothesis is advanced that obviously brings into a direct sequence of cause and effect all the phenomena of human history, we must accept it, and if we accept we must teach it. The mere fact that it overthrows social organizations cannot affect our attitude. The rest of society can reject or ignore, but we must follow the new light no matter where it leads. Only about two hundred and fifty years ago the common sense of mankind, supported by the authority of revealed religion, affirmed the undoubted and self-evident fact that the sun moved round the earth. Galileo suddenly asserted and proved that the earth moved round the sun. You know what followed, and the famous "E pur si muove." Even if we, like Galileo, should be obliged by the religious or secular authority to recant and repudiate our science, we should still have to say as he did in secret if not in public, "E pur si muove."

Those of us who have reached or passed middle age need not trouble ourselves very much about the future. We have seen one or two great revolutions in thought and we have had enough. We are not likely to accept any new theory that shall threaten to disturb our repose. We should reject at once, and probably by a large majority, a hypothetical science that must obviously be incapable of proof. We should take the same attitude that our fathers took toward the theories and hypotheses of Darwin. We may meantime reply to such conundrums by the formula that has smoothed our path in life over many disasters and cataclysms: "Perhaps the crisis will never occur; and even if it does occur, we shall probably be dead." To us who have already gone as far as we set out to go, this answer is good and sufficient, but those who are to be the professors and historians of the future have got duties and responsibilities of a heavier kind than we older ones ever have had to carry. They cannot afford to deal with such a question in such a spirit. They would have to rejoin in Heine's words:

> Also fragen wir beständig,
> Bis man uns mit einer Handvoll
> Erde endlich stopft die Mäuler,
> Aber is das eine Antwort?

They may at any time in the next fifty years be compelled to find an answer, "Yes" or "No," under the pressure of the most powerful organizations the world has ever known for the suppression of influences hostile to its safety. If this association should be gifted with the length of life that we all wish for it, a span of a century at least, it can hardly fail to be torn by some such dilemma. Our universities, at all events, must be prepared to meet it. If such a crisis should come, the universities throughout the world will have done most to create it, and are under most obligation to find a solution for it. I will not deny that the shadow of this coming event has cast itself on me, both as a teacher and a writer; or that, in the last ten years, it has often kept me silent where I should once have spoken with confidence, or has caused me to think long and anxiously before expressing in public any opinion at all. Beyond a doubt, silence is best. In these remarks, which are only casual and offered in the paradoxical spirit of private conversation, I have not ventured to express any opinion of my own; or, if I have expressed it, pray consider it as withdrawn. The situation seems to call for no opinion, unless we have some scientific theory to offer; but to me it seems so interesting that, in taking leave of the association, I feel inclined to invite them, as individuals, to consider the matter in a spirit that will enable us, should the crisis arise, to deal with it in a kindly temper, and a full understanding of its serious dangers and responsibilities.

Ever truly yours,

HENRY ADAMS.

HERBERT B. ADAMS, Esq.,
    Secretary, etc., American Historical Association.

A LETTER TO AMERICAN TEACHERS OF
HISTORY

1910

A LETTER TO AMERICAN TEACHERS OF HISTORY

1603 H Street,
Washington, D. C.

Dear Sir:

Availing myself of the privilege commonly granted, in the liberal professions, to age and seniority, I use the freedom of an old colleague in offering this small volume for your acceptance.

Some fifteen years ago, on retiring from the Presidency of the Historical Association, I made a short address on the relations of the Historical Department to society; and, had such a custom existed, I should have gladly enlarged the paper to the dimensions of a Report. The volume now sent you, is, in effect, such a Report, unofficial and personal.

Touching, as it does, some of the most delicate relations of University Instruction in rival departments, the book has too much the air of provoking controversy. I do not know that controversy would do harm, but I see nothing to be gained by provoking it. For the moment, the problem is chiefly one of technical instruction; of grouping departments; at most, of hierarchy in the sciences. Some day, it may become a question whether one department, or another, is to impose on the University a final law of instruction; but, for the present, it is a domestic matter, to be settled at home before inviting the world to interfere. Therefore, the volume will not be published, or offered for sale, or sent to the press for notice.

For the same reason, the volume needs no acknowledgment. Unless the questions which it raises or suggests seem to you so personal as to need action, you have probably no other personal interest than that of avoiding the discussion altogether. Few of us are required to look ten, or twenty years, or a whole generation ahead, in order to realize what will then be the relation of history to physics or physiology, and even if we make the attempt, we are met at the outset by the difficulty of allowing for our personal error, which is, in so delicate a calculation, an element of the first importance. Commonly, our personal error takes the form of inertia, and is more or less constant and calculable. For myself, the preference for movement of inertia is decided. The risk of error in changing a long-established course seems always greater to me than the chance of correction, unless the elements are known more exactly than is possible in human affairs; but the need of determining these elements is all the greater on that account; and this volume is only a first experiment towards calculating their past, present and future values.

Mathematicians assume the right to choose, within the limits of logical contradiction, what path they please in reaching their results, provided that when they come to the end of their process, they consent to test their result by the facts of experience. More than this cannot fairly be asked of historians.

If I call this volume a letter, it is only because that literary form affects to be more colloquial or more familiar than the usual scientific treatise; but such letters never require a response, even when they invite one;

and in the present case, the subject of the letter involves a problem which will certainly exceed the limits of a life already far advanced, so that its solution, if a solution is possible, will have to be reached by a new generation.

16 FEBRUARY, 1910.

CHAPTER I

THE PROBLEM

THE mechanical theory of the universe governed physical science for three hundred years. Directly succeeding the theological scheme of a universe existing as a unity by the will of an infinite and eternal Creator, it affirmed or assumed the unity and indestructibility of Force or Energy, as a scientific dogma or Law, which was called the Law of the Conservation of Energy. Under this Law the quantity of matter in the universe remained invariable; the sum of movement remained constant; energy was indestructible; "nothing was added; nothing was lost;" nothing was created, nothing was destroyed.

Towards the middle of the nineteenth century, — that is, about 1850, — a new school of physicists appeared in Europe, dating from an Essay on the Motive Power of Heat, published by Sadi Carnot in 1824, and made famous by the names of William Thomson, Lord Kelvin, in England, and of Clausius and Helmholz in Germany, who announced a second law of dynamics. The first law said that Energy was never lost; the second said that it was never saved; that, while the sum of energy in the universe might remain constant, — granting that the universe was a closed box from which nothing could escape, — the higher powers of energy tended always to fall lower, and that this process had no known limit.

The second law was briefly stated by Thomson in a paper "On a Universal Tendency in Nature to the Dissipation of Mechanical Energy," published in October, 1852, which is now as classic as Kepler's or Newton's Laws, and quite as necessary to a scientific education. Quoted exactly from Thomson's "Mathematical and Physical Papers" (Cambridge, 1882, Vol. I, p. 514), the Law of Dissipation runs thus : —

"1. There is at present in the material world a universal tendency to the dissipation of mechanical energy.

"2. Any restoration of mechanical energy, without more than an equivalent of dissipation, is impossible in inanimate material processes, and is probably never effected by means of organized matter, either endowed with vegetable life or subjected to the will of an animated creature.

"3. Within a finite period of time past, the earth must have been, and within a finite period of time to come, the earth must again be, unfit for the habitation of man as at present constituted, unless operations have been, or are to be performed, which are impossible under the laws to which the known operations going on at present in the material world, are subject."

When this young man of twenty-eight thus tossed the universe into the ash-heap, few scientific authorities took him seriously; but after the first gasp of surprise physicists began to give him qualified support which soon became absolute. "This conclusion made much noise," says Ostwald ("L'Énergie," Paris, 1910); "the more because Helmholz and Clausius gave in their adherence to it. We owe to the latter the following formula: 'The Entropy of the Universe tends toward a maximum.'" To physicists, this law of Entropy became "a prodigiously abstract conception," according to the familiar phrase of M. Poincaré; but to the vulgar and ignorant historian it meant only that the ash-heap was constantly increasing in size; while the public understood little and cared less about Entropy, and the literary class knew only that the Newtonian universe, in which they had been cradled, admitted no loss of energy in the solar system, where the planets, at the end of their planetary years, returned exactly to their positions at the beginning. Gravitation showed no waste of energy whatever, except where friction occurred, but had planets gone off like comets, and never returned, the scholar of 1860 would still have feared to question the scientific dogma which asserted resolutely, without qualification, the fact that nothing in nature was lost. If no other assurance had satisfied him, all doubts were silenced by the famous outburst of eloquence with which Tyndall concluded his Lectures in 1862, on "Heat as a Mode of Motion." Old men can still recall how, after explaining that "the quantity of the solar heat intercepted by the earth is only $\frac{1}{2,300,000,000}$ of the total radiation," Tyndall refrained from telling what became of the heat not intercepted by the earth, and went on to expatiate with enthusiasm on the unity of the universe and its energy : —

"Look at the integrated energies of our world, — the stored power of our coalfields ; — our winds and rivers ; — our fleets, armies and guns ! What are they ? They are all generated by a portion of the sun's energy which does not amount to $\frac{1}{2,300,000,000}$ of the whole. This, in fact, is the entire fraction of the sun's force intercepted by the earth, and in reality we convert but a small fraction of this fraction into mechanical energy. Multiplying all our powers by millions of millions, we do not reach the sun's expenditure. And, still, notwithstanding this enormous drain, in the lapse of human history we are unable to detect a diminution of his store. Measured by our largest terrestrial standards, such a reservoir of power is infinite; but it is our privilege to rise above these standards, and to regard the sun himself as a speck in infinite extension, — a mere drop in the universal sea. We analyse the space in which he is immersed, and which is the vehicle of his power. We pass to other systems and other suns, each pouring forth energy like our own, but still without infringement of the law which reveals immutability in the midst of change, which recognises incessant transference and conversion, but neither final gain nor loss. This law generalises the aphorism of Solomon, that there is nothing new under the sun, by teaching us to detect everywhere, under its infinite variety of appearances, the same primeval force. To nature nothing can be added; from nature nothing can be taken away; the sum of her energies is constant, and the utmost man can do in the pursuit of physical truth, or in the application of physical knowledge, is to shift the constituents of the never-varying total, and out of one of them to form another. The law of conservation rigidly excludes both creation and annihilation. Waves may change to ripples and ripples to waves, — magnitude may be substituted for number, and number for magnitude, — asteroids may aggregate to suns, suns may resolve themselves into floræ and faunæ, and floræ and faunæ melt in air, — the flux of power is eternally the same. It rolls in music through the ages, and all terrestrial energy, — the manifestations of life as well as the display of phenomena, are but the modulations of its rhythm."

This magisterial tone irritated some of the new physicists to the point of hinting that Tyndall deliberately misstated the facts of physics, for fear lest some one should drive him into a logical snare, ending in the necessity of admitting a Creation. In flat contradiction to Tyndall, Kelvin and Tait affirmed that "the same primeval force" could never be detected, — much less recovered; that all nature's energies were slowly converting themselves into heat and vanishing in space, until, at the last, nothing would be left except a dead ocean of energy at its lowest possible level, — say of heat at 1° Centigrade, or — 272° C. below freezing point of water, — and incapable of doing any work whatever, since work could be done only by a fall of tension, as water does work in falling to sea-level.

Between such authorities the unscientific student could not interfere. Naturally, all his sympathies were with Tyndall. The idea that the entire sidereal universe could have gone on for eternity dissipating energy, and never restoring it, seemed, at the least, unreasonable; while

L

the astronomers drew up lists of nebulæ by hundreds in the very act of generating universes, and the geologists showered the theory with rocks in order to show that the sun had already reached an age many times greater than Thomson was willing to allow it.

No one knew, although every one explained what had caused the inequalities of energy; least of all could the historian of human society assert or deny that energy could be created or could not be destroyed. The subject was beyond his province. Since the Church had lost its authority, the historian's field had shrunk into narrow limits of rigorously human action; but, strictly within those limits, he was clear that the energy with which history had to deal could not be reduced directly to a mechanical or physico-chemical process. He was therefore obliged either to deny that social energy was an energy at all; or to assert that it was an energy independent of physical laws. Yet how could he deny that social energy was a true form of energy when he had no reason for existence, as professor, except to describe and discuss its acts? He could neither doubt nor dispute its existence without putting an end to his own; and therefore he was of necessity a Vitalist, or adherent of the doctrine that Vital Energy was independent of mechanical law. Vitalists are of many kinds.

"In former times a special force was adduced, — the force of life. More recently when many phenomena of plant life had been successfully reduced to simple chemical and mechanical processes, this vital force was derided and effaced from the list of natural agencies. But by what name shall we now designate that force in nature which is liable to perish while the protoplasm suffers no physical alteration? . . . This force in nature is not electricity or magnetism; it is not identical with any other natural force, for it manifests a series of characteristic effects which differ from all other forms of energy. Therefore I do not hesitate again to designate as 'vital force' this natural agency, not to be identified with any other, whose immediate instrument is the protoplasm, and whose peculiar effects we call life. The atoms and molecules of protoplasm only fulfil the functions which constitute life so long as they are swayed by this vital force." ANTON KERNER, "The Natural History of Plants."

Students who are curious on the subject can consult the "Vitalismus als Geschichte und als Lehre," by Dr. Hans Driesch (Leipzig, 1905); but they will understand it little better afterwards than before. For human history the essential was to convince itself that social energy, though a true energy, was governed by laws of its own.

To the generation of Lord Macaulay and George Bancroft, the problem seemed scarcely serious. They could ignore the dispute, since Thomson agreed with Tyndall so far as to admit that, for human purposes, the Dissipation of Solar Energy was so slow as to be indistinguishable from Conservation of Energy. The historian never even took the trouble to inform himself of the bearings of the problem. Indeed at that time, the Universities showed a nervous unwillingness to teach philosophy at all, and were especially averse to all philosophies of history, whether inspired by Hegel or by Comte, by Buckle or by Karl Marx. The law that history was not a science, and that society was not an organism, calmed all serious effort; and historians turned to the collection of facts, as the geologists turned to the collection of fossils. For them it was a happy period, and literature profited by it.

In fact, the problem was by no means simple, and the historian might have made himself a very competent professor of Physics without the smallest profit to history. Kelvin's law asserted the constant dissipation of energy, but the process was far more complex than appeared in this statement. Energy had a way of coming and going in phases of intensity much more mysterious than the energy itself. Catastrophe was its law. The sun, according to Tyndall, wasted into space practically all its energy except an imperceptible portion that happened to fall on the earth; but even this portion was not utilizable, for human purposes, to boil a pint of water, at sea-level, without assistance. Ice, water, and vapor were phases sharply distinct. So the imperceptible portion of solar energy which fell on the earth, reappeared by some mysterious process, to an infinitely minute measure, in the singular form of intensity known as Vital Energy, and disappeared by a sudden and violent change of phase known as death. Man had always flattered himself that he knew — or was about to know — something that would make his own energy intelligible to itself, but he invariably found, on further inquiry, that the more he knew, the less he understood. Vital energy was, perhaps, an intensity; — so, at least, he vaguely hoped; — he knew nothing at all!

No one knew anything; and yet the analogy between Heat and Vital Energy, suggested by Thomson in his Law of Dissipation, — and received by the public with sleepy indifference, — was insisted upon by the physicists in accents that became sharper with every generation, until it began to pass the bounds of scientific restraint. Already in 1884, Faye, in his "Origin of the World," fairly threatened mankind with its doom: —

"We must therefore renounce those brilliant fancies by which we try to deceive ourselves in order to endow man with unlimited posterity, and to regard the universe as the immense theatre on which is to be developed a spontaneous progress without end. On the contrary, life must disappear, and the grandest material works of the human race will have to be effaced by degrees under the action of a few physical forces which will survive man for a time. Nothing will remain : — '*etiam periere ruinæ!*'"

Thus, it seemed, that whatever the universities thought or taught, the physicists regarded society as an organism in the only respect which seriously concerned historians : — It would die! If life was to disappear, the form of Vital Energy known as Social Energy, must also, presumably, go to increase the Entropy of the Universe, thus proving — at least to the degree necessary and sufficient to produce conviction in historians, — that History was a Science. Although Faye settled this point, as a matter of thermodynamics, as early as 1884, his successors in authority have gone on repeating it with increasing energy of expression ever since. To these outbursts of prophecy the story will have to recur, but for the moment, the only point requiring insistence is that sixty years of progress in science have only intensified the assertion that Vital Energy obeys the law of thermal energy. The sketch of Kelvin's Life and Work by Professor Andrew Gray, —

Professor of Natural Philosophy in the University of Glasgow, — published in 1908, renews the warning in almost angry terms. Once more he asserts, as an axiom of physics, that all work is done by conversion of one energy, or intensity, into another, and a lower : — "If this conversion is prevented, all processes which involve such conversion must cease, and among these are vital processes. . . . It will be the height of imprudence to trust to the prospect, not infrequently referred to, at the present time, of drawing on the energy locked up in the atomic structure of matter. . . . After a large part of the whole existent energy has gone to raise the dead level of things, no difference of temperature, adequate to work between, will be possible, and the inevitable death of all things will approach with headlong rapidity."

This may serve to represent the very last opinion of physicists. The latest expression of metaphysics, — for the present purpose, — shall be taken from the notes added by Eduard von Hartmann to the last edition of his works, dated in 1904 : —

"If the social consciousness of to-day rebels so strongly against the thought that vital processes will come to an end in the world, the chief reason is because society has indeed absorbed the first principle of thermodynamics, — the conservation of energy, — but not the second, the progressive degradation of energy by dissipation and levelling of intensities; and, in consequence, has erroneously interpreted the first law as though it contained an eternal guaranty of the endlessness of vital processes. . . . In reality, the only question is whether, in the actual result, the world-process will work itself out slowly in prodigious lapse of time, according to purely physical laws; or whether it will find its end by means of some metaphysical resource when it has reached its culminating point. Only in the last case would its end coincide with the fulfilment of a purpose or object; in the first case, a long period of purposeless existence would follow after the culmination of life." (Ausgewählte Werke, vIII, pp. 572–573. Leipzig, 1904.)

Thomson's famous paper on "A Universal Tendency in Nature to the Dissipation of Energy" was published in 1852. Seven years afterwards, Charles Darwin announced his law of Evolution, which involved a contradiction, — as von Hartmann implies, — to both the laws of thermodynamics. Thomson, physicist and mathematician, had thought only of providing the energy necessary to move his world; Darwin, neither physicist nor mathematician, took the necessary energy as given. Possibly, if he thought about it at all, he assumed the Law of Conservation as the mechanical equivalent of

Lyell's Law of Uniformity; but he seemed scrupulously careful to avoid asserting either principle. On his own account he never committed himself to the doctrine that, within the geological record, organization had largely advanced, or risen to higher powers, but he did assert, and permitted his followers to assert much more broadly that "the inhabitants of the world, at each successive period in its history, have beaten their predecessors in the race for life, and are, in so far, higher in the scale"; meaning probably that they were better fitted to their conditions, but conveying the idea that their vital powers had risen from lower to higher by the spontaneous struggle of the organism for life. This popular understanding of Darwinism had little to do with Darwin, whose great service, — in the field of history, — consisted by no means in his personal theories either of natural selection, or of adaptation, or of uniform evolution; which might be all abandoned without affecting his credit for bringing all vital processes under the law of development or evolution, — whether upward or downward being immaterial to the principle that all history must be studied as a science.

Society naturally and instinctively adopted the view that Evolution must be upward; and Haeckel performed the feat of measuring the height of each step from protozoa up to man; but still without further attempt to account for the source or the nature of the numerous energies implied in the process of elevation. Apparently he felt no need of invoking any energy beyond that of uniform solar heat, and took for granted the power of all organisms to rise in potential by its absorption.

Thus, at the same moment, three contradictory laws of energy were in force, all equally useful to science: — 1. The Law of Conservation, that nothing could be added, and nothing lost, in the sum of energy. 2. The Law of Dissipation, that nothing could be added, but that Intensity must always be lost. 3. The Law of Evolution, that Vital Energy could be added, and raised indefinitely in potential, without the smallest apparent compensation.

Although the physicists are far from clear in defining the term Vital Energy, and are exceedingly timid in treating of Social Energy, they are positive that the law of Entropy applies to all vital processes even more rigidly than to mechanical. "Thus it is," says Ostwald ("L'Énergie," Paris, 1910, p. 116), "that animated beings always grow old, and never young." As the point is pivotal for evolution, it must be understood as admitted in the Law of Degradation. One of the latest authorities, M. Dastre, professor of physics at the Sorbonne, in his volume called "La Vie et la Mort" (Paris, 1902), lays down the dogma in one line : — "Vital Energy ends as its last term, in thermal Energy." He admits that this rule is too absolute ; it has exceptions ; but the exceptions are not serious : —

"The cycle of energy ends occasionally in mechanical energy (movement), and in some smaller degree, in other energies, as for example, in the electric energy produced by nervous action and the muscles in all animals ; or in functions of special organs, as in the rays, torpedoes, and thunder-fish ; or finally in the luminous energy of phosphorescent animals ; but these are secondary matters." The essential is that the second law of thermodynamics rules biology with an authority fully as despotic as it asserts in physics. "If chemical energy is the generative maternal form of the vital energies, calorific energy is the form of waste (déchet), of excrement ; the form which is degraded, according to the expression of the physicists. . . . In the animal organism, heat is transformed into nothing : it is dissipated" (p. 109). "The animal world expends the energy which the vegetable world has accumulated." The vegetable world draws its energy from the sun, and "the animals end by restoring it, in the form of dissipated heat, to the cosmic space."

This teaching is explicit. Animal energies accent and

emphasize the law of physics that nature, always and everywhere, tends to an equilibrium by levelling its intensities. Mechanical energies admit apparent exceptions, like gravitation, but animal energies admit none. All grow old and die. This is the teaching of physics, and although most physicists show caution in defining exactly what they mean by vital energy, the law, as they announce it, is relentless. For human purposes, whatever does work is a form of energy, and since historians exist only to recount and sum up the work that society has done, either as State, or as Church, as civil or as military, as intellectual or physical, organisms, they will, if they obey the physical law, hold that society does work by degrading its energies. On the other hand, if the historian follows Haeckel and the evolutionists, he should hold that vital energy, by raising itself to higher potentials, without apparent compensation, has accomplished its work in defiance of both the laws of thermodynamics.

Down to the end of the nineteenth century nothing greatly mattered, since the actual forces could be fairly well calculated or accounted for on either principle, but schools of applied mechanics are apt to get into trouble by using contradictory methods. One process or the other acquires an advantage. The weaker submits, but in this instance, the difficulty of naming the weaker was extreme. That the Evolutionist should surrender his conquests seemed quite unlikely, since he felt behind him the whole momentum of popular success and sympathy, and stood as heir-apparent to all the aspirations of mankind. About him were arranged in battalions, like an army, the energies of government, of society, of democracy, of socialism, of nearly all literature and art, as well as hope, and whatever was left of instinct, — all striving to illustrate not the Descent but the Ascent of Man. The *hostis humani generis*, the outlaw and enemy, was the Degradationist, who could have no friends, because he proclaimed the steady and fated enfeeblement and extinction of all nature's energies; but that he should abandon his laws seemed a still more preposterous idea. Never had he asserted them so aggressively, or with such dogmatic authority. He held undisputed possession of every technical school in the world, and even the primary schools were largely under his control. His second law of thermodynamics held its place in every text-book of science. The Universities and higher branches of education were greatly, if not wholly, controlled by his methods. The field of mathematics had become his. He had no serious intellectual rival. Few things are more difficult than to judge how far a society is looking one way and working in another, for the points are shifting and the rate of speed is uncertain. The acceleration of movement seems rapid, but the inertia, or resistance to deflection, may increase with the rapidity, so that society might pass through phase after phase of speed, like a comet, without noting deflection in its thought. If a simpler figure is needed, society may be likened to an island surrounded by a rising ocean which silently floods its defences. One after another the defences have been abandoned, and society has climbed to higher ground supposed to be out of danger. So the classic Gods were abandoned for monotheism, and scholastic philosophy was dropped in favor of the Newtonian; but the classic Gods and the scholastic philosophy were always popular, and the newer philosophies won their victories by developing compulsory force. Inertia is the law of mind as well as of matter, and inertia is a form of instinct; yet in western civilization it has never held its own.

The pessimism or unpopularity of the law will not prevent its enforcement, if it develops superior force, even if it leads where no one wants to go. The proof is that the law is already enforced in every field excepting that of human history, and even human history has not wholly escaped. In physics it rules with uncontested sway. In physiology, the old army of Evolutionists have suffered defections so serious that no discipline remains. A full account of the situation would need an amount of knowledge that is now granted to no one; but the most trifling popular science is enough for popular teachers like ourselves.

Every one knows that Darwin owed much of his science as well as of his success to Sir Charles Lyell, who supplied him with the doctrine of uniformity and the evidence to support it. Darwin's own assumptions or theories were quite sufficiently difficult of proof, without adding the doctrine of uniformity; but Sir Charles' ability and authority carried the point in spite of Kelvin's protest that uniformity could not be admitted as possible under the second law of thermodynamics. Lyell's conservative system of evolution, resting on several broad assumptions of fact, became not merely a physiological, but even more a philosophical dogma, and in a literary point of view the Victorian epoch rested largely, — perhaps chiefly, — on the faith that society had but to follow where science led; to —

> "Move upward, working out the beast,
> And let the ape and tiger die";

in order to attain perfection. An infinite series of imperceptible steps, continuous under uniform conditions since the earliest traces of organic life, and always tending upwards to higher intensities, — tensions, — potentials, — according to the growing complexity of the organism, had already taken the place of religious dogma, and bridged the gap between two phases of thought.

With a sense of vast relief, the generation which began life in 1850, embraced the new creed, not so much because it was proved, as because it was convenient; but it met with instant difficulties on the side of the Darwinists themselves. The warmest evolutionists were the least confident, not only about adaptation and the struggle for existence, but also, and chiefly, about uniformity. Heer's researches on the arctic flora, already cited by Sir Charles Lyell in the tenth edition of his "Principles" (London, 1867), seemed to upset the law of uniformity from top to bottom and to substitute a sweeping law of catastrophe; so that already in 1879, Saporta, in his History of the World of Plants, asserted that nothing less than absolute revolution in cosmic conditions could account for the changes in northern vegetation. During the whole period since the eocene, the temperature of the planet had steadily declined. "The phenomenon to which the lowering of temperature must be referred," said Saporta, "is in no way peculiar to Europe; it has nothing sudden about it, or accidental, or transient. We pointed out its origin at the end of the eocene; we have marked its progress by its increasing intensity in the polar regions, and by its gradual extension thence towards the south. At the beginning of the oligocene, the vegetation of the northern temperate zone changes character; new elements, coming from the north, and marking the first progress of a refrigeration, introduce and propagate themselves. We have studied the signs of this revolution, by means of which the differences of latitude tend little by little to accentuate themselves. . . . It is impossible not to admit, when we consider this march which nothing stops, and which continues with moderation and regularity, the influence of a cosmic phenomenon embracing the terrestrial globe altogether" (p. 322). The inference followed : — "We recognize from this point of view as from others, that the world was once young; then adolescent; that it has even passed the age of maturity; man has come late, when a beginning of physical decadence had struck the globe, his domain." ("Le Monde des Plantes," p. 109.)

Nothing could be more fatal, not to Darwin but to Darwin's popular following. As Newton said that he was never a Newtonian, so Darwin might perhaps have said that he was never a Darwinian, but his popular influence lay in the law that evolution had developed itself in unbroken order from lower to higher. Kelvin

M

had indeed, flatly contradicted this assumption of fact, but had done so from the physicist's point of view, as a matter of solar heat and terrestrial cooling; while Saporta's studies of vegetation, to everybody's astonishment, so dramatically confirmed Kelvin's mathematics that, though the two streams of thought continued to flow in opposite directions, Saporta already in 1878 had the courage to incline to the "bold suggestion made some years ago by Dr. Blandet, and approved by the late M. d'Archiac," to the effect that, in times before the cretaceous, — especially well shown in the extravagance of the carboniferous, — the sun equaled the orbit of Mercury in diameter. The long epochs known as the Permian, Triassic, Jurassic, Cretaceous and Eocene allowed ample time for shrinkage before the Miocene first proved by its temperate vegetation, that the sun had approached its present diameter, and could no longer equably warm the world.

Such an adhesion to the law of thermodynamics, only twenty years after Darwin and Lyell had established their system on the law of Conservation, seemed to strike a very serious blow at the theory of upward evolution as the world understood it. The violent contradiction between Kelvin's Degradation and Darwin's Elevation was so profound, — so flagrant, — so vital to mankind,

that the historian of human society must be supposed to
have watched with agonized interest the direction which
science should take; since the decision of palaeontologists
would fatally decide his own. If they should adhere to
the high authority of Saporta, the biologists must follow;
and then the historian of man would find himself facing
a responsibility such as had never before entered into his
imagination.

Thirty years have passed since Saporta published his
"Monde des Plantes avant l'Apparition de l'Homme,"
and a whole generation has indefatigably collected, discussed, published and re-discussed the evidences, with results recorded in a library of books and in a score of great
geological museums. With the truths that have been established or the theories that have been proposed, historians
need trouble themselves little, or not at all, further than to
ask what theories are to-day actually taught or are accepted
by standard authorities. For American purposes, the
object is best reached by restricting the inquiry to the last
ten or fifteen years, and, as far as possible, to the schools of
the European continent, because distance makes both
teachers and teaching impersonal. Beginning with France,
the standard authority in geology is said to be Lapparent's
Treatise (3 vols. Paris, 1906), and to this the inquirer turns
to ask whether Darwin's ideas, or Kelvin's, have pre-

vailed in the French schools. The answer is easily
found : —

"If there is one fact," says Lapparent (Vol. III, p.
1951), "that palaeontology, and especially the branch of
that science which concerns the vegetable world, has put
in strong evidence, it is assuredly the progressive diminution of heat in the high latitudes of our globe." Among
a number of explanations suggested, none satisfied all
the conditions except that of M. Blandet, — the diminution of the apparent diameter of the sun. "Outside of
this conception, the maintenance of the solar heat is
absolutely inexplicable (p. 1954). . . . One cause alone,
according to the laws of thermodynamics, is capable of
preserving the solar energy without appealing to the quite
inadequate help of outside sources ; — this is the phenomenon of condensation in the sun. By the means of such
condensation, the calorific power of the sun is able to
maintain itself without sensible loss, by means of a lessen-
ing of apparent diameter which would need several
thousand years to become perceptible to our most delicate
apparatus. . . . But if, in our days, the sun, reduced as it
is, undergoes still this movement of concentration necessary to maintain its energy, what must have been the difference of its dimensions at other epochs from what they
are now? Nothing is more logical than this hypothesis,

and since, — while irreproachable from the astronomic point of view, — it is alone adequate to explain the palaeo-thermal phenomena, we think we cannot do better than propose it for the adhesion of geologists."

Nothing could be more innocent in intention, or at least in appearance, than this adhesion to the second law of thermodynamics, — this harmonizing of several great branches of science, — this unifying of nature; but its consequences to the old law of Evolution and to the school of Darwin were beyond disguise. Lapparent went on to indicate some of them, and first the necessary abandonment of Lyell's law of uniformity : —

"Let us content ourselves, then, with indicating the possibility of this solution, while affirming, contrary to the doctrines of the uniformitarian school, that the ancient history of our planet has unrolled itself in the midst of external conditions very different from those which now surround us."

While Lapparent offered this theory of solar shrinkage as only a possible solution, other geologists were working on a corollary to the theory, which has become one of the commonest foundations of their teaching. Solar shrinkage might perhaps be suggested as a doubtful possibility, but terrestrial shrinkage, which rests on the same law, seems to be now commonly admitted as a reasonably orthodox dogma. Yet terrestrial shrinkage is a mere derivative, which involves solar shrinkage as its logical and mathematical concomitant. If adopted as a fundamental law of geology, it must be admitted as a fundamental law of solar physics, since the one is as inseparable from the other as a Siamese twin. Naturally the theory is not conceded to be true; — no theory is; — but it is convenient; it is taught; and the chance is now small that any geological physicist will forego the temptation of using M. Blandet's theory as law.

Fortunately for the old school of geologists, — as well as for all schools of historians, — the few certainties of geology as of history are so easily read in opposite senses, that, in practice, every teacher can teach — and ignore — what he pleases. Pure geologists still adhere more or less strictly to the uniformitarian creed and reject the conclusions of Heer and his followers. Geological physicists still teach that if the second law of thermodynamics controlled all history from the gaseous nebula to the glacial epoch, it has certainly controlled the few days or years since the ice-cap retired from the Niagara river. In that case, man became the most advanced type of physical decadence, no longer at the top but at the bottom of the ladder, in face of accelerated extinction.

At what precise moment the sun reached, under this

theory, the equilibrium which gave the utmost exuberance
to organic life, only a specialist can venture to say; but,
from the language of their text-books, a reader gathers
that the energy of vegetable growth is supposed to have
reached its climax as early as the carboniferous, —
"période de luxe, s'il en fut jamais" (Saporta, 73); —
and that when this amazing vegetation lost its wonderful
power, as shown in the coal-formations (Lapparent, II,
1027), it was followed by an equally astonishing animal
growth which lasted into the miocene period. There —
we are told, — degradation began! At the end of the
miocene, both vegetable and animal forms of life are
declared to offer proof that the poles could no longer support their previous exuberance. This teaching assumes
that the equable temperature, whether high or low, which
had prevailed from the poles to the equator gave place
to climatic differences consequent on the sun having
shrunk towards its present diameter. Nature instantly
showed the shrinkage of energy. "In spite of the multitude of beings which have disappeared at different epochs,"
says Gaudry ("Essai," 44), "I think that the sum of
appearances exceeded that of extinctions down to the end
of the miocene period." The steady decline continued
until the convulsion of the glacial epoch, when, in the midst
of a wrecked solar system, man suddenly appeared.

"Since this great event occurred," according to Lapparent (III, 1655), "the organic world has enriched itself with no new species, but several forms have disappeared, among those that surrounded the first men; and the great herbivorous mammals, already on their decline, have seen their principal representatives, little by little, quit the scene of the world."

This statement, as a mere statement of fact, seems to be accepted as rather unduly mild; but not yet satisfied with admitting that organic geology, like inorganic, confirms the dissipation of energy down to the present day, M. Lapparent, abandoning all hope that the process can ever be reversed, concludes (III, 1961): "If any new term is still to be looked for, it seems as though none could be imagined other than an era where the Soul, freed from the bonds of matter, should dominate. Except for this hope there are none but sombre perspectives in sight for all that surrounds us. The progress of the emersion of boreal lands seems destined to extend from step to step the influence of the polar ice. The sun, whose condensation is already far advanced, will soon find in the narrowing of its diameter no sufficient source for maintaining its heat, and large spots will appear on its surface, destined to transform themselves into a dark shell. The day when the extinction of the central luminary shall be complete, no further physical or physiological reaction can take place on our globe, which will then be reduced to the temperature of space, and the sole light of the stars. But, perhaps, before arriving there, the globe will have lost its oceans and its atmosphere, absorbed in the pores and fissures of a shell whose thickness will increase from day to day."

If one, and by far the most extensive period of terrestrial history, is already taught in this sense by physicists, all biology, including human history, will have also to be re-edited by them according to this lugubrious plan; and the University professor of history as it has been hitherto understood, will soon have urgent need to make up his mind whether to accept or resist it. If he decides to accept it, he has only to hold his tongue, and remain quietly in the pleasant meadows of antiquarianism, protected as heretofore by the convenient and sufficient axiom of the nineteenth century that history is not a science, and society not an organism; but if this resource should fail him, his first thought will be to find allies. He will seek them among his Darwinist friends, to begin with; but he will scarcely finish the opening chapter of the last book on Transformation, Mutation, Inheritance, or whatever new name may, as one writer expresses it, dissimulate creative or destructive force under the term

Evolution, without discovering that the familiar, genial dispute over the origin of species has turned into a sinister and almost lurid battle over the extinction of species, for which the Darwinian theories of survival are declared inadequate to the point of childishness.

In the place of minute variations extending over indefinite time under uniform conditions, he will find that views have been put prominently forward which bear an alarming resemblance to the second law of thermodynamics. So, one palaeontologist,—Dollo,—formulated in 1893 the law of evolution in three sections, each a contradiction to the old law. — 1. Development has proceeded by leaps. — 2. It is irreversible. — 3. It is limited. Another authority, Rosa, gave new form to an old idea, by showing how variability proceeds according to a law of progressive reduction ; — that is to say, every series of forms is destined to extinction according to the degree of its specialization. Even if this law were not rigorously exact, "it is perfectly exact to say that the number and extent of variations diminishes as the specialization advances." The reader, who marks with some nervousness that Man has certainly advanced by leaps, and that his progress seems to be irreversible, seeks at once to know whether he shows signs of reaching its limit; and, for an answer, appeals to the only scientific source of information, — the anthropologist.

Unless the inquirer is full of courage, he will be aghast at the confusion of responses which his prayer disturbs. Yet he knows, if he is an evolutionist, that Darwinians have always had trouble over the origin and end of Man. To Darwin and Haeckel the difficulties were as great as to their successors. The mystery of man was then, and still remains, a scientific scandal which has inevitably roused bad temper, and sometimes bad manners, even in the centres of science itself. Every investigator in turn evaded, with more or less dexterity, — or broke through, with more or less recklessness, — the difficulties that surrounded him; but the difficulties outlived the explanations. The first and most notorious was due to the fact that, while the strict theory of evolution from lower to higher made it reasonable to assume that man was descended from that group of animals which resembled him most, and while there was no doubt that the nearest group which could be supposed to lead up to him was that of the anthropoid ape, the anthropologists instantly found so many scientific objections to this line of ascent that it had to be abandoned from the start. The skull of the young anthropoid, it appeared, had more resemblance than that of its adult parent, to the skull of man; in other words, the anthropoid might be a degraded man, but man could not be a developed anthropoid. The search would have to go much further back, to find some earlier mammal with less resemblance to man, and therefore with fewer evidences of descent, and less probability of satisfying the rules of evidence. Each step in the ascent added enormously to the difficulties of proof.

Every evolutionist knows how disastrously this first failure affected anthropology; nor was the case bettered for the anthropologist by Cope, who, reasoning from the teeth, made man descend from an eocene lemur, and through him from the marsupials, without passing through any known group of anthropoids at all; — a leap backwards covering such vast epochs of unknown time and change, — only to end in a type much lower than that of the despised apes, — as to have no more value for human history than though, instead of a hypothetical lemur, the palaeontologists had offered as an ancestor a hypothetical lingula of archean time.

All this fumbling for an ancestry that should have been self-evident, was sufficiently disconcerting to historians who cared little what kind of a pedigree was given them, but greatly wanted to be sure of it; and who found themselves embarrassed with a primitive man, — or probably a variety of primitive men, — running back without intermediate links to a hypothetical, primitive, eocene lemur, whom no one but a trained palaeontologist could distinguish from a hypothetical, primitive opossum, or weasel or squirrel or any other small form of what is commonly known as vermin. For the historian, the lemur was a grievance. It offered no foundation for any theory, whether of conservation, elevation, or degradation, physical or moral. Even the Church had always admitted as sound doctrine that God might have used more or less consecutive types for his creations; but between the hypothetic lemur and the talking man, no type, consecutive or other, existed for God to use.

The historian had certainly a right to complain of this Pharaonic command to adopt a lemurian and marsupial ancestry, including the duck-billed platypus, and much more; but had he rashly attempted to seek further, he might probably have found worse. Indeed, from the moment when science had exhausted the whole geological series, — recent, pleistocene, pliocene, miocene, oligocene, and part of the eocene, — without coming upon any reasonable or respectable ancestor at all, the search had become, for the historian's purposes, worse than futile. He would do much better to fall back on the mere hope that his own historical parentage was lost under the polar snows, — like the carboniferous forests, — where some happier anthropoid had been born and bred in temperate miocene luxury, to be driven southward before the ice-cap

which obliterated every trace of him and of his polar Eden
as he slowly drifted towards the fortieth parallel. Such
a vague but aristocratic origin would relieve him from
quartering the arms of the lemur, and might help him
to suppress the opossum.

Hoping for the best, he next turns to the last text-
book, — say Hopf's "Human Species" (London, 1909),
— and first notes that it still rests the chief weight of the
argument, as Cope did, on the teeth, but in a sense that
startles even a sincerely convinced evolutionist. Among
the first authorities quoted is Professor Klaatsch of Heidel-
berg : — "As in his opinion, man by no means stands at
the head of all living beings with respect to all parts of
his organization, so too he considers that the human
teeth are among the most primitive possessed by any of
the existing mammals. Had man not sacrificed twelve
teeth in the course of his gradual development, he would
now have forty-four, the highest number possessed by any
land-dwelling mammal." Assuredly, according to actual
standards of physical beauty, a man — and still more a
woman — with forty-four teeth would raise scruples
about the law of evolution from lower to higher; but
the Professor evidently regards the modest number of our
actual teeth as a decadence; and goes on to say that
even as to his molars, man "has not progressed beyond

the stage of development reached by the mammals in the tertiary period." Not a step have the physiologists advanced in thirty years towards proof of any rise in vital energy. Greatly concerned at this evidence of feebleness in the evolution of man from the eocene lemur, the historian of human society naturally asks what human senses show more development than is proved by the teeth. Hopf makes no pretence of flattery even on this point. "Speaking generally, man, not only in a state of civilization, but also the primitive savage, — the Papuan, for example, — has a much less acute sense of smell than that possessed by animals" (Hopf, 240). Finally, though discouraged, the historian probably inquires in what, then, the evolution of man from lower to higher is believed to consist; and he learns that it consists in the extraordinary development of the brain, with its instruments, the hand, the foot, and the vocal organs; but even the brain is said to show extremely slight real differences from that of the higher monkeys (Vulpian, "Leçons," 1866). "The brain has passed through evolution in all the branches of the tree of mammals; it is highly circumvoluted at the extremity of certain branches; sometimes the richness of its circumvolutions exceeds that of Man" (Topinard, 334); but its only marked development is in weight, and in number of ganglion cells (Hopf, 168).

Inevitably the puzzled historian asks almost stupidly whether the anthropologist holds this increase of brain to prove evolution from lower to higher, and he receives an answer that totally demoralizes him. The weight of the brain is not asserted to be a gauge of its energy. Neither instinct nor reason is supposed to have any relation to the weight of the brain; on the contrary, "in a list of seventeen brains, the heaviest known, going from 1729 to 2020 grams, there are seven lunatics," and only three men of science, about whose degree of aberration no exact statistics can be reasonably expected (Topinard, 216).

This is only the beginning of anthropological evolution from lower to higher. The anthropologist seems inclined to hold that what is called genius has no relation with weight of brain; but that, even though it had, it would not help evolution, if Arndt is right in asserting that superior mental endowment of any kind is a sign of degeneration; or if Branca is right in thinking it impossible that the progressive enlargement of the human brain can go on indefinitely without enfeebling the body till it dies out; or if Hopf is right (p. 374), in admitting that, in civilized races, increase in intellectual power often goes with a narrowing of the jaw and an early loss of the teeth, and of the hair, and in women with an inability to suckle their children. To complete the picture, the anthropologist who hesitates to say in what sense the brain should be regarded as proving evolution from lower to higher, shows not the least sign of doubt in regard to the degree to which Man is specialized, particularly as shown by his brain, his hand, his foot, and his vocal organs. In fact, according to Louis Agassiz, man is "the last term of a series beyond which, following the plan on which the whole animal kingdom is built, no further progress is materially possible" ("De l'Esprit," p. 34), and is, therefore, under Rosa's law of progressive reduction, destined to be rapidly extinguished.

Thus the physical geologist has frankly and finally gone over to the side of Kelvin; the palaeontologist has kept him company, or even went before him; while the anthropologist is somewhat painfully hesitating, obedient to the physicists, but trying to remain true to humanity, though acutely conscious that the two directions cannot be reconciled. For many years M. Topinard has held a sort of position as semi-official anthropologist of France, but he has become incoherent with age, finding himself caught between the irreconcilable contradictions of science and sentiment: — "The end, as far as concerns us, we know," he says in his last volume ("L'Anthropologie," Paris, 1900); "our earth will cease to be

N

habitable; it will grow cold; will lose its atmosphere and its moisture, and will resemble our actual moon. Previously, evolution, from progressive will become stationary, then regressive. Some day, as Huxley suggests, the lichens, the diatomaceae, the protococcus, will perhaps be the only beings adapted to the conditions; — then, nothing!" The picture seems sad enough, yet M. Topinard might have added that, according to his own palaeontologist authorities, the evolution of life on the earth had ceased to be progressive some millions of years ago, and had passed through its stationary period into regression before man ever appeared; while M. Topinard himself adds (pp. 321, 370) that, "to his stupefaction," he has reached conclusions of his own which seem, to readers who do not take these opinions too seriously, exceedingly like an admission that he finds himself an example of the second law of thermodynamics: —

"Yes! there is contradiction between the animal man, — as he was in a state of nature, and as he has maintained himself to our day, — and the social man such as he ought to be. Yes! the objective realities of science are in contradiction with the subjective aspirations of man. Yes! nature laughs at our conceptions. Society has been born of man, and has been built on sand, often with only materials of convention. The individual for whom it is created is always its worst enemy; he admits it, but will not bend to its necessities."

Although M. Topinard adhered blindly to the second law of thermodynamics in regard to the approaching end of the world, and was logically obliged to accept its conclusion that all useful work or progress, social or mechanical, depended on inequalities of intensity, endowed with energy still left to dissipate, the moment he realizes that such inequalities still exist, and that therefore progress is still possible, he bewails the fact as an inexplicable and unfortunate mystery. Such cross-purposes have become almost a standard rule in sociology. They have always been the rule in history.

In the earlier scientific commentaries on the Law of Dissipation, astronomers and physicists commonly took some little pains to soften the harshness of their doom by assurances that the prospect was not so black as it seemed, but that the sun would adapt itself to man's convenience by allowing some thousands or millions of years to elapse before its extinction. This pleasing thoughtfulness has vanished. Geologists, when most generous, scarcely allow more than thirty thousand years since the last ice-cap began its partial recession; while, quite commonly, they insist that their most careful and elaborate estimates do not justify them in granting more than a quarter of that time to the very incomplete process of clearing away the ice and snow from the streets of primitive New York and Boston. The cataclysmic ruin that spread over all the most populous parts of the northern hemisphere while the accomplished and highly educated architects of Nippur were laying the arched foundations of their city, has, it is true, been partially covered or disguised under new vegetation; but even this brief retrospective reprieve is darkened by the earnest assurances of the most popular text-books and teachers that they can hold out no good reason for hoping that the exemption will last. The sun is ready to condense again at any moment, causing another violent disequilibrium, to be followed by another great outburst and waste of its expiring heat.

The humor of these prophecies seldom strikes a reader with its full force in America, but in Europe the love of dramatic effect inspires every line. Compared with the superficial and self-complacent optimism which seems to veneer the surface of society, the frequent and tragic outbursts of physicists, astronomers, geologists, biologists, and sociological socialists announcing the end of the world, surpass all that could be conceived as a natural product of the time. The note of warning verges on the grotesque; it is hysterically solemn; a little more, and it would sound like that of a Salvation army; a small natural shock might easily turn it to a panic. Naturally a historian is most interested in what concerns primitive history, and all the relations of primitive man to nature. He takes up the last work on the subject, which happens in 1910, to be "Les Premières Civilisations," by M. J. de Morgan, published in June, 1909. M. de Morgan is one of the highest authorities — possibly quite the highest authority — on his subject, and this volume contains the whole result of his vast study. Unconscious of thermodynamics, he treats primitive man as a sort of function of the glacial epoch, and ends by telling his readers (p. 97) : —

"The glacial period is far from being ended ; our times, which still make an integral part of it, are characterized by an important retreat of the glaciers, started long before the beginnings of history. It is to be supposed that this retreat of the ice is not definitive, but that the cold will return, and with it the depopulation of a part of our globe. Nothing can enable us to foretell the amplitude of this future oscillation, or the lot which the laws of nature destine to humanity. During this cataclysm revolutions will occur which the most fecund imagination cannot conceive, — disasters the more horrible because, while the population of the earth goes on increasing every day, and even the less favored districts little by little become inhabited, the different human groups, crowded back one on another, and finding no more space for existence, will be driven to internecine destruction."

M. de Morgan belongs to the most serious class of historians, while M. Camille Flammarion, the distinguished director of the Meudon observatory, besides being a serious astronomer, is also one of the most widely read, and most highly intelligent, vulgarizers of science. When he reaches the point of describing the solar catastrophe in his popular astronomy, he lays bare an enormous field for harrowing horrors ("Astronomie Populaire," 102, 103, Paris, 1905) : —

"Life and human activity will insensibly be shut up within the tropical zones. Saint Petersburg, Berlin, London, Paris, Vienna, Constantinople, Rome, will successively sink to sleep under their eternal cerements. During many centuries, equatorial humanity will undertake vain arctic expeditions to rediscover under the ice the sites of Paris, of Bordeaux, of Lyons, of Marseilles. The sea-shores will have changed and the map of the earth will be transformed. No longer will man live, — no longer will he breathe, — except in the equatorial zone, down to the day when the last tribe, already expiring in cold and hunger, shall camp on the shores of the last sea in the rays of a pale sun which will henceforward illumine an earth that is only a wandering tomb, turning around a useless light and a barren heat. Surprised by the cold, the last human family has been touched by the finger of death, and soon their bones will be buried under the shroud of eternal ice. The historian of nature would then be able to write : — 'Here lies the entire humanity of a world which has lived! Here lie all the dreams of ambition, all the conquests of military glory, all the resounding affairs of finance, all the systems of an imperfect science, and also all the oaths of mortals' love! Here lie all the beauties of earth!' — But no mortuary stone will mark the spot where the poor planet shall have rendered its last sigh!"

As though to assure the public that he knows what he is talking about, M. Flammarion, who is a practical astronomer, goes on with a certain sombre exaltation, like a religious prophet, to say that the terrors he predicts are of common occurrence in astronomy, and leaves his scholars to infer that nature regards her end as attained only when she has treated man as an enemy to be crushed : —

"Already we have seen twenty-five stars sparkle with a spasmodic light in the heavens, and fall back in extinction neighboring death! Already some of the brilliant stars hailed by our fathers have disappeared from the charts of the sky, and a great number of red stars have entered into their period of extinction!"

Volumes would be needed if a writer should attempt to follow the track of this idea through all the branches of present thought; but, without unnecessarily disturbing the labors of anthropology and biology, the merest insect might be excused for asking what happens to fellow insects, who, like himself, are enjoying the precarious hospitality of these numerous solar systems. M. de Morgan and M. Flammarion are contented with freezing them; but M. Lapparent takes the loftier view that they will do better to become disembodied spirits; which is even less likely to suit either the American professor or the American student, whose ideas of education are exceptionally practical. The "soul, freed from the bonds of matter," seems to require no education unless in the passive consciousness of pure mathematics and logic, which has hitherto been the weakest side of the American student, who is averse even to the ingenuous simplicity of logarithms and vectors. More than this, the law of degradation inexorably implies that, throughout the whole series of phases which may intervene in the future as in the past, in the dissipation of the higher intensities, a sympathetic exhaustion must be expected in all the energies dependent on the central system, among which, as the palaeontologists and physicists have assured us, the vital energies are not only the most dependent, but also and particularly the most sensitive. Physical or mental, they should, according to theory, suffer an accelerated decline, and yet their actual position should also show a certain lag behind the rate of the central energy. They are really worse off than they seem. The soothing vision of thousands or millions of years, for the ultimate extinction of solar energy, protects the Universities to a highly inadequate degree from their own extinction in the process. All energies which are convertible into heat must suffer degradation; among these, as the physicists expressly insist, are all vital processes; the mere temporary approach to a final equilibrium would be fatal; and, among all the infinite possibilities of evolution, the only absolute certainty in physics is that the earth every day approaches it. No one can be trusted to express so much as an opinion about the moment when any special vital process may expect to be reduced in energy; man and beast can, at the best, look forward only to a diversified agony of twenty million years; but at no instant of this considerable period can the professor of mathematics flatter either himself or his students with an exclusive or extended hope of escaping imbecility.

According to some geologists, this view is extravagantly

— almost ridiculously — optimistic; but with the scientific correctness of these opinions, the historian is not concerned. He asks only how far the teaching of his colleagues contradicts his own, and how far society sides with his contradictors. His question is difficult to answer. At first sight he is conscious of no divergence. ⌈Society has the air of taking for granted its indefinite progress towards perfection with more confidence, and sometimes with more dogmatism than in 1830, when Macaulay made it a literary law by his famous polemic against Southey. Yet the same society has acquired a growing habit of feeling its own pulse, and registering its own temperature, from day to day; of prescribing to itself new régimes from year to year; and of doubting its own health like a nervous invalid. Granting that the intended effect of intellectual education is, — as Bacon, Descartes, and Kant began by insisting, — a habit of doubt, it is only in a very secondary sense a habit of timidity or despair. To a certain point, the more education, the more hesitation; but beyond that point, confidence should begin. Keeping Europe still in view for illustration and assuming for the moment that America does not exist, every reader of the French or German papers knows that not a day passes without producing some uneasy discussion of supposed social decrepitude; — falling off of the birth-rate; — decline of rural population; — lowering of army standards; — multiplication of suicides; — increase of insanity or idiocy, — of cancer, — of tuberculosis; — signs of nervous exhaustion, — of enfeebled vitality, — "habits" of alcoholism and drugs, — failure of eye-sight in the young, — and so on, without end, coupled with suggestions for correcting these evils such as remind a historian of the Lex Poppaea and the Roman Empire rather than they prove that careless confidence in itself which ought to stamp the rapid rise of social energy which every one asserts and admits. A great newspaper opens the discussion of a social reform by the axiom that "there are unmistakable signs of deterioration in the race." The County Council of London publishes a yearly volume of elaborate statistics, only to prove, according to the London *Times*, that "the great city of to-day," of which Berlin is the most significant type, "exhibits a constantly diminishing vitality"; and, in almost the same breath, other journals exult in showing that the globe is rapidly becoming a suburb of the great cities. Rarely does the press dwell on proofs of social evolution except as shown negatively in decline of the death-rate, or of illiteracy, or in relief from pain, and never does the statistician or sociologist help the historian to any clear understanding of the progress expected as his literary goal.

The medical profession is singularly shy of pledges. The poets are pessimists to a man — and to a woman. The legislators pass half their time, in Germany, France, and England, framing social legislation, of which a large part rests on the right and duty of society to protect itself against itself, not under the fiction of elevating itself from lower to higher, but — as in the case of alcohol and drugs — to protect itself from deterioration by the exercise of powers analogous to the power of war.

According to the sociologists, the most serious symptom of all is the extension of philosophical schools founded on the supposed failure of society : — "The formation of these great systems is the sign that the pessimist current has reached an abnormal degree of intensity due to some perturbation of the social organism. Now we all know how they have multiplied in our day. To get a just idea of their number and their importance, we have to consider not merely the philosophies which officially profess that character, like those of Schopenhauer, von Hartmann, etc., but we must also take account of all those which, under different names, are the results of the same spirit. The anarchist, the esthete, the mystic, the revolutionary socialist, even if they do not despair of the future, agree with the pessimist in the same sentiment of hatred and disgust for whatever is; in the same need of destroying

the real, and escaping from it. The collective melan-
choly would not have invaded consciousness to that point
unless it has taken morbid development; and in consequence the development of suicide which results from it,
is of the same nature. All the proofs unite in causing us
to regard the enormous increase which has shown itself
within a century in the number of voluntary deaths, as
a pathological phenomenon which becomes every day
more menacing." — EMILE DURKHEIM, "Le Suicide."
Paris, 1897.

As yet the press is alarmist with decency, even in Paris
and Berlin, but at the rate of progress since 1870, the
press might soon learn to blacken the prospects of humanity with all the picturesque genius of Camille Flammarion.
A little more superficial knowledge is all it needs; the
general disposition is already excellent. Meanwhile,
the teacher of history has fallen out of sight. The
freedom that was liberally extended to others was denied
to him. Supposing Kelvin's law, with Lapparent's conclusions, and Flammarion's illustrations, to be rigorously
true, and that its truth was admitted in biology as in
physics, the American professor who should begin his
annual course by announcing to his class that their year's
work would be devoted to showing in American history
"a universal tendency to the dissipation of energy" and

degradation of thought, which would soon end in making America "improper for the habitation of man as he is now constituted," might not fear the fate of Giordano Bruno, but would certainly expect that of Galileo, even though he knew that every member of the Cardinals' College of professors held the same opinion. The University would have to protect itself by dismissing him.

The truth or the error of the three Laws of Evolution does not properly concern the teacher. No physicist can, in these days, be expected to take oath that Dalton's atoms, or Willard Gibbs' phases, or Bernouilli's kinetic gases, are true. He uses for his scholars the figure or the formula which best suits their convenience. The historian or sociologist is alone restricted in the use of formulas which shock the moral sense; yet the stoppage of discussion in the historical lecture-room cannot affect the teaching of the same young men in the physical laboratory, — still less the legislation of their parents at the State capital; it would merely ruin the school of history. However much to be regretted is such a result, society cannot safely permit itself to be condemned to a lingering death, which is sure to tend towards suicide, merely to suit the convenience of school-teachers. The dilemma is real; it may become serious; in any case it needs to be understood.

The battle of Evolution has never been wholly won;
the chances at this moment favor the fear that it may yet
be wholly lost. The Darwinist no longer talks of Evolution; he uses the word Transformation. The historian
of human society has hitherto, as a habit, preferred to
write or to lecture on a tacit assumption that humanity
showed upward progress, even when it emphatically
showed the contrary, as was not uncommon; but this
passive attitude cannot be held against the physicist who
invades his territory and takes the teaching of history
out of his hands. Somewhere he will have to make a
stand, but he has been already so much weakened by the
surrender of his defences that he knows no longer where
a stand can be made. As a form of Vital Energy he is
convicted of being a Vertebrate, a Mammal, a Mono-
delphe, a Primate, and must eternally, by his body, be
subject to the second law of thermodynamics. Escape
there is impossible. Science has shut and barred every
known exit. Man can detect no outlet except through
the loophole called Mind, and even to avail himself of
this, he must follow Lapparent's advice, — become a disembodied spirit and seek a confederate among such
physicists or physiologists as are willing to admit that
man, as an animal, has no importance; that his evolution
or degradation as an organism is immaterial; that his

physical force or condition has nothing to do with the subject; that the old ascetics were correct in suppressing the body; and that his consciousness is sufficient proof of his right to regard Reason as the highest potential of Vital Energy.

The historian, thrown back on this oldest of battle-grounds, may console himself with the thought that the physicists and physiologists are as much embarrassed as himself; but while, in former ages, the world went on, after a fashion, trusting to the energy of its archaic instincts to make good the lapses of its reasoning powers, the external pressure of physical forces, under their thermodynamic laws, seems of late to have literally driven physical science into an assumption of universal authority, so that physiologists can no longer evade the logical necessity of framing a stem-history for the mind, as for the body or the skeleton; and since their law tends strongly towards monism, — unity of energy, — they cannot supply man with any other energies or laws than he inherited from his only known — or unknown — ancestor, the hypothetical eocene lemur. In the system of *Energetik*, Reason can be only another phase of the energy earlier known as Instinct or Intuition; and if this be admitted as the stem-history of the Mind as far back as the eocene lemur, it must be admitted for all forms of

Vital Energy back to the vegetables and perhaps even to the crystals. In the absence of any definite break in the series, all must be treated as endowed with energy equivalent to will.

The idea is very familiar in philosophy; the strangeness consists in its gaining foothold in science. At the Congress of the Italian Society for the Progress of Sciences held at Parma in 1907, Ciamician, the distinguished Professor of the University of Bologna, suggested that the potential of Vital Energy should be taken as the Will. The step seems logical, and to the historian it seems natural. The idea is as old as Aristotle; any one who cares to study its history will find it in Eduard von Hartmann's "Philosophie des Unbewussten" (Vol. II, pp. 426–439, Leipzig, 1904); but, for the actual uses of to-day, the story goes back no further than to Schopenhauer's famous work, "Die Welt als Wille," which appeared in 1819–1844. Schopenhauer held that all energy in nature, latent, or active, is identical with Will. Before his time, — he claimed, — the concept of Will was included in the concept of Force; he reversed the order on the ground that the unknown should be referred to the known, and that therefore the whole universe of energy, known or unknown, of whatever intensity or volume, should be brought into the category of intuition.

O

The philosophers, even when rejecting the identity of Will with Energy, were before long busily coquetting with the idea, which offered extraordinary charms to inventors of systems. For the historian, Schopenhauer's method had the double merit of logically merging the two great historical schools of thought. The old idea of Form, which ruled the philosophy of Aristotle and Thomas Aquinas, slipped readily over the idea of Energy, taught by Kelvin and Clausius, so that henceforward it mattered little whether the schools, in their rage for nomenclature, called the result "Will," or "Entelechy," or "Dominant," or "Organic Principle," or "Trieb," or "Strebung," or "Intuition," or "Instinct," or just simply "Force" as of old; even the forbidden words "Creative power" became almost orthodox science; in any case the logic of "Will" or "Energetik" imperatively required that every conception whatever, involving a potential, obliged ontologists to regard the will-power of every stem as the source of variation in the branches, and to admit, as a physical necessity, that the branch which has lost the power of variation should be regarded as an example of enfeebled energy falling under the second law of thermodynamics.

Such an arrangement, however convenient for degradationists, and however tempting to students of palaeon-

tology in particular, is likely to bring trouble on other
branches of education. Especially for human history
its bearings are painfully pointed. Already the anthropologists have admitted man to be specialized beyond
the hope of further variation, so that, as an energy, he
must be treated as a weakened Will, — an enfeebled
vitality, — a degraded potential. He cannot himself
deny that his highest Will-power, whether individual or
social, must have proved itself by his highest variation,
which was incontrovertibly his act of transforming himself from a hypothetical eocene lemur, — whatever such
a creature may have been, — into a man speaking an
elaborately inflected language. This staggering but self-
evident certainty requires many phases of weakening
Will-power to intervene in the process of subsidence into
the reflective, hesitating, relatively passive stage called
Reason; so that in the end, if the biologists insist on im-
posing their law on the anthropologists, while at the same
time refusing to admit a break in the series, the historian
will have to define his profession as the science of human
degradation. The law of thermodynamics must embrace
human history in its last as well as in its earliest phase.
If the physicist can suggest any plausible way of escaping this demonstration, either logically or by mathematics, he will confer a great benefit on history; but,

pending his decision, if the highest Will-power is conceded to have existed first, and if the physicist is to be granted his postulate that height and intensity are equivalent terms, while fall and diffusion are equivalent to degradation, then the intenser energy of Will which showed itself in the primitive extravagance of variation for which Darwin tried so painfully to account by uniformitarian formulas, must have been — and must be now in the constant process of being — degraded and lost, and can never be recovered. The process, in physics, is not reversible.

If the historian of human society is to let himself be placed in this position, the fact should be understood and accepted in advance. In that case, two schools of history can be easily organized; but the effect on other branches of instruction is not so simple. Ciamician's suggestion, — like Schopenhauer's, like Nietzsche's, like Eduard von Hartmann's philosophy, — does, no doubt, threaten human history with fantastic revolution, but perhaps its strangest result is that of converting metaphysics into a branch of physics. Nothing in the history of philosophy is more distinctly marked than the effort of physics and metaphysics, since 1890, to approach each other. Only a specialist knows even the titles of the books on this subject, in the German language alone; but a beginner might perhaps try to get an idea of the process from Wilhelm Wundt's well-known "System der Philosophie" (Leipzig, 1897). The naturalist now readily admits that plants have souls — or will-power, — but he appropriates the soul as an energy of thermodynamics. At first sight, the tendency seems towards metaphysics, but the true current is the reverse. The chaos is more chaotic than ever, but the effort to make the laws of *Energetik* cover all, is perhaps the only very vigorous intellectual activity now in evidence.

Both parties have in consequence appealed to the Psychologists, and, under the lead of Ostwald in Germany and of Loeb in America, have created, within the last few years, a new literature so extensive as to defy all students except advanced specialists. Indeed, almost as in mathematics, the specialist himself is rarely equal to his task. Every country in the world is contributing to the pursuit of psychological laws. In Russia, Krainsky's volume on the "Law of Conservation of Energy applied to Psychical Activity" appeared as long ago as the year 1897. The amount of intelligence and patient research put into the investigation is as great as though wealth were its end; and, though the drift of evidence may seem to a historian both clear and strong, he has, as yet, no right to hamper the inquiry by inflicting on these exceedingly clever and earnest seekers any inquiries of his own. At most, in his desperate search for allies to protect him from the tyranny of thermodynamics, he might timidly ask, not them but himself, whether the new psychology tends towards the possibility that Reason may be a more or less remote consequence of Tropism, — that is to say, a form of motion excited by exterior forces. In itself, this old and very familiar theory, that "nous vivons parce que nous sommes excités," is as indifferent to sociologists as any other physico-chemical or mechanical analogy used for purposes of technical instruction; but if it goes to the point of asserting, as an acquired truth, that the motion of the mind is an induced motion which follows the laws of electricity, the historian of mind in its social variety will find himself seriously embarrassed. Without going back to the earlier discussion of this burning question, an inquirer may allow himself to quote the latest form in which the distinguished chief of the school states it. Ostwald says : — "Between psychological and mechanical operations, there seems to be nearly the same difference and the same resemblance, as between electric and chemical operations " ("L'Énergie." Paris, 1910, p. 210). On this question, Loeb is even a higher authority than Ostwald, and his latest expressions are still more emphatic. He recognizes no such thing as Will: — "It seems to me," he says, "that it is in the interest of psychology itself to favor the development of the theory of tropisms"; and not of tropisms alone; — "My object is to refer psychical phenomena not only to tropisms but also to physico-chemical phenomena" ("La Revue des Idées," October 15, 1909). With the utmost ingenuity and labor he has proved that, at least in many low organisms, what is taken for Will is really mechanical attraction.

Loeb's demonstrations are quite beautiful pieces of work which rouse high admiration for his powers; but their bearing on his colleagues is obscure. If Thought is capable of being classed with Electricity, or Will with chemical affinity, as a mode of motion, it seems necessarily to fall at once under the second law of thermodynamics as one of the energies which most easily degrades itself, and, if not carefully guarded, returns bodily to the cheaper form called Heat. Of all possible theories, this is likely to prove the most fatal to Professors of History.

The dilemma is pointed out by Dr. Hanna Thomson, in his book on the Brain, with the emphasis that suits its tension: — "Physically the gap between the brain of man and the brain of an anthropoid ape is too insignificant to count; but their difference as beings corresponds to the distance of the earth from the nearest fixed star. The brain of man does not account for man? What does?"

The question, thus bluntly posed, is bluntly answered in a sense hostile to the physicist law. The brain is developed by the Will, which lies within and behind the brain : — "By practice . . . the Will-stimulus will not only organize brain-centres to perform new functions, but will project new connecting, — or, as they are technically called, association — fibres, which will make nerve-centres work together as they could not, without being thus associated." The motive-power is not of the brain, "because it is the masterful personal Will which makes the brain human" by developing one of the brain-hemispheres; and "this Something known as Will," continues Dr. Hanna Thomson, "is not natural, but supernatural, both in its powers and in its creations."

Of course the supernatural character of the Will is the whole point in dispute, and the usual doctrine of the modern psychologist substitutes the word Nature for the word Supernatural. Thus Paul Flechsig, concluding his address to the Psychological Congress in Rome (1905), says that "only by constant, progressive changes in the physical form of the brain, has Nature succeeded in attaining this truly lofty end. Thus the Will shows organic evolution from first to last, and shows in this respect no difference from other bodily functions. It is a product of organic nature, and, at least in its broadest sense, bears that stamp."

The three views seem far apart, and yet one can conceive that Kelvin, who troubled himself only with the practical means of obtaining a fall of potential equivalent to the work done, might have seen no necessary contradiction to his law in either case : —

"Quite so !" he might be supposed to reply; "the force that Thomson calls supernatural Will, and Flechsig calls an organic function, and Loeb calls a physicochemical relation, is the force which I call vital Energy, and which I agree with Dr. Thomson in regarding as supernatural in the sense that nature no longer produces it here, more than she produces any other element or atom. Physicists are at perfect liberty to regard the Will as another name for the same primitive, elementary, unexplained energy which gave odor to a molecule of copper, or made the magnolia burst into flower with more than animal sensuality and perfection of form, color, scent, and line; or the caterpillar suddenly soar into the air with the amazing, inconceivable sensual properties of the butterfly; but the mere brain-mechanism you talk about is, in physics, far less extraordinary, as Will, than what went before it, — creations always growing higher in tension as you go backward, — like the eye, or the innumerable varieties or transformations of the shapes which vital energy has taken in every province of the vegetable and animal kingdoms, while all are still subordinate and even trivial when compared with the primary creation of energy itself, about which no one knows anything except its name, — Nature."

The professor of physics will be shocked at seeing such words put into Kelvin's mouth. In that case Kelvin's own words will answer almost equally well: "Science positively affirms creative power. . . . Modern biologists are coming once more to a firm acceptance of something beyond mere gravitational, chemical, and physical forces; and that unknown thing is a vital principle. . . . We are absolutely forced by science to admit and to believe with absolute confidence in a directive power. . . . There is nothing between absolute scientific belief in creative power, and the acceptance of the theory of a fortuitous concourse of atoms. Just think of a number of atoms falling together of their own accord, and making a crystal, a sprig of moss, a microbe, a living animal!" (Life, 1098.)

Such reasoning in circles helps the historian little to make headway against the current of physical energies.

His dilemma remains untouched. The physicist says that Thought is an organic growth which has the faculty of determining its own action within certain limits, but whose "Freedom" exists only in the atmosphere of ideals. By the majority of physiologists, Thought seems to be regarded — at present — as a more or less degraded Act, — an enfeebled function of Will : —

"Thought comes as the result of helplessness," says Lalande in his volume on "Dissolution" (Paris, 1899. p. 166) ; "Thought, as Bain says, is the refraining from speech or action. The truth is, therefore, that action comes first ; the idea is an act which tends to accomplish itself, and which, when stopped by some obstacle before its realization, finds a new form of reality in that stoppage. Jean Jacques Rousseau said : 'The man who thinks is a depraved animal' ; and in this he expressed an exact view of psychology. As far as he is animal, the thinker is a bad animal ; eating badly ; digesting badly ; often dying without posterity. In him the degradation of vital energy is flagrant. (La dépravation de la nature physique est visible chez lui.)"

The late volume of M. Bergson, "L'Evolution Créatrice," is the most widely known among the very latest efforts of metaphysicians .to defend their conceptions against the methods of physics ; and yet, on this point of

Reason and Instinct, M. Bergson seems ready to go further than M. Lalande. The whole chapter on Instinct ought to be read, and studied in connection with the treatment of the same subject by Reinke, in his "Einleitung" (Kap. 21), and the source of it all in Eduard von Hartmann's "Unbewusste;" but a few paragraphs will serve to express the present views of the Collège de France about the relative value of phases of life as forces : —

"From our point of view, life appears globally as an immense wave which starts from a centre to propagate itself outwards, and which is arrested at almost every point of its circumference, and is converted into oscillation without advance; at one point alone, it has forced the obstacle, and the impulse has passed on freely. This liberty is registered in the form of man. Everywhere except with man, consciousness has been brought to a stop; with man alone it has pursued its road. . . . In doing so, it is true, it has abandoned not merely the baggage that embarrassed it, but has been obliged to renounce also some precious properties. Consciousness, in man, is chiefly intelligence. It might have been, — it seems as though it ought to have been, — intuition too. . . . Another evolution might have led to a humanity either still more intelligent, or more intuitive. In reality, in the humanity of which we make part, intuition is almost completely sacrificed to intelligence. . . . Intuition is still there, but vague, and especially discontinuous. It is a lamp, almost extinguished, which gains strength at long intervals, where a vital interest is at hazard, but only for a few instants. On our personality, on our liberty, on the place we occupy in nature as a whole, on our origin, and perhaps also on our destiny it casts a feeble and flickering light, but a light which pierces, none the less, the darkness of the night in which our intelligence leaves us" (pp. 288–289).

If this is the best that physiology and metaphysics can do to help the historian of man, the outlook is far from cheerful. The historian is required either expressly to assert, or surreptitiously to assume, before his students, that the whole function of nature has been the ultimate production of this one-sided Consciousness, — this amputated Intelligence, — this degraded Act, — this truncated Will. As the function of the crystal is to produce the order of its cleavage, and that of the rose, the beauty of its flower, and that of the peacock, the splendors of its tail, and as, except for these purposes, neither crystal, rose nor peacock has as much human interest as a thistle or a maggot, so the function of man is, to the historian, the production of Thought; but if all the other sciences affirm that not Thought but Instinct is the potential of

Vital Energy, and if the beauties of Thought — shown in the intuitions of artistic genius, — are to be taken for the last traces of an instinct now wholly dead or dying, nothing remains for the historian to describe or develop except the history of a more or less mechanical dissolution. The mere act of reproduction, which seems to have been the most absorbing and passionate purpose of primitive instinct, concerns history not at all, except as the botanist is concerned with the question whether the flower is a developed or degraded leaf ; but the question whether the plant exists to produce the flower, or to produce the leaf, is vital. The University, as distinct from the technological school, has no proper function other than to teach that the flower of vital energy is Thought, and that not Instinct but Intellect is the highest power of a supernatural Will ; — an ultimate, independent, self-producing, self-sustaining, incorruptible solvent of all earlier or lower energies, and incapable of degradation or dissolution.

Intellect should bear the same relation to Instinct that the sun bears to a gaseous nebula, and hitherto in human history it has asserted this relation without a doubt of its self-evident truth. The assertion has led to physical violence and intellectual extravagance without limit, so that history shows man as alternately insane with his own pride of intellect, and shuddering with horror at its bloody consequences; but the remains of primitive instinct taught society that it could not abandon its claim to be, or to represent, a supernatural and independent energy, without, by the same act, admitting and demonstrating its progressive enfeeblement of will. If Intellect led to such an abdication, it proved the universal truth of the second thermodynamic law.

From the beginnings of philosophy and religion, the thinker was taught by the mere act of thinking, to take for granted that his mind was the highest energy of nature. Society still believes it, and asserts its supremacy, on no other ground, with a sustained force which is the chief theme of history, and which showed no sign of relaxation until attacked in the eighteenth century in its theological or supernatural outposts. Society must still continue to act upon it, as the Platonist, the Stoic and the Christian did, for the obvious reason that it was and is their only motive for existence, — their solitary title to their identity.

History has never regarded itself as a science of statistics. It was the Science of Vital Energy in relation with time; and of late this radiating centre of its life has been steadily tending, — together with every form of physical and mechanical energy, — towards mathematical expression. The torrent of physical energy has swept society into its course, until every school, and almost every teacher in the world, — except perhaps in the Church, — takes an attitude of instinctive and silent hostility to any form of energy that claims to be independent. Even though the triumph of this teaching is the ultimate degradation of the energy that is taught, — of the teacher as well as of the pupil and the universe, — and the more complete his victory, the more rapid his degradation, the fault is not his that the radiating centre of his world should betray this visible decline of vigor.

Very unwillingly can he admit Reason to be an energy at all; at the utmost, he can hardly allow it to be more than a passive instrument of a physico-chemical energy called Will; — an ingenious economy in the application of power; a catalytic medium; a dynamo, mysteriously converting one form of energy into a lower; — but if persuaded to concede the intrinsic force of Reason, he must still reject its independence. As a force it must obey the laws of force; as an energy it must content itself with such freedom as the laws of energy allow; and in any case it must submit to the final and fundamental necessity of Degradation.

The same law, by still stronger reasoning, applies to the Will itself.

CHAPTER II

The Solutions

THE general reader, though apt to mistake the drift of thought, is still rather a better judge of it than the specialist can be, and he gets, from the literature of the twentieth century in its first decade, a decided impression that educational energy has passed into the hands of the physico-chemists and teachers of *Energetik* or thermodynamics. The old Law of Conservation, or mechanics, still rules in the workshop, but is somewhat lifeless in the scholars if not in the schools. Its teachers seem rather inactive, or even indifferent; yet possibly, here and there, one of them may feel uneasy at the prospect of actually coming to blows with his brother-professors as in the old days of religion. The Law of Conservation was an easy one; it left a reasonable share of freedom in the universe; even astronomers were allowed to be devout, and sometimes actually were so; while in strictness, physicists cease to be physicists unless they hold that the law of Entropy includes Gods and men as well as universes. Nevertheless even a physicist may occasionally bear in patience with perfectly impartial, and, though conservative, yet not unsympathetic bystanders, who try to act as though the door were still open, and who beg only to be told what the new physicists are willing to do for mankind. What mankind will do for itself is quite another matter, since probably all teachers admit that, in daily life, society may go on indefinitely, quite as well, — or as ill, — in the future as in the past; but as between schools of education the divergence is wide. Possibly the Universities may think it safer to ignore the dilemma for another decade or two, as they have ignored so many others; but they would do better to reach an understanding if they can, especially because, if both parties could be brought into some slight sacrifice of principle, and so abate the rigor of their law, the compromise might put new life into the school of history, which badly needs it.

For purposes of teaching, the figure is alone essential, and the figure of Rise and Fall has done infinite harm from the beginnings of thought. That of Expansion and Contraction is far more scientific, even in history. Evolution, again, is troublesome, and has already yielded to the less compromising figure of Transformation. Expansion and Transformation are words which commit teachers to no inconvenient dogma; indeed, they are so happily adapted for Galileos who are wise enough not to shock opinion, that they seem to impose themselves on the lecture-room. In strictness, no doubt, water which falls and dynamite which expands, are equally degraded energies, but the mind is repelled by the idea of degradation, while it is pleased by the figure of expansion. Because an energy is diffused like table-salt in water, it is not rendered less useful; on the contrary, it can only by that process be made useful at all to an animal like man whose life is shut within narrow limits of intensity; who sends for a physician if his temperature rises a single degree, and who dies if it rises or falls 5° Centigrade; whose bath must be tempered and his alcohol diluted; and whose highest ambition is to train and temper his own brute energies to obey law. Notoriously civilization and education enfeeble personal energy; *emollit mores:* they aim especially at extending the forces of society at cost of the intensity of individual forces. "Thou shalt not," is the beginning of law. The individual, like the crystal of salt, is absorbed in the solution, but the solution does work which the individual could not do.

Put in this form the law of thermodynamics seems less obnoxious. With the change of one word to another, the most sensitive evolutionist might not refuse a hearing to the physicist who should affirm that organic as well as inorganic nature shows a universal tendency to the dissipation of energy. At the utmost, the Evolutionist would need only to point out that nature, contrary to her usually wasteful habits, often teaches extreme economy, as when she locks up her energies in atoms and molecules, or, what is more to man's purpose, when she trains the glow-worm to habits of costless industry that may well make the sun veil its face; but, consenting to pass over, for the moment, this restriction on thermodynamic extravagance, the Darwinian will perhaps for the sake of harmony, concede that, however economical the process may be in its details, dissipation of energy is always occurring in the mass, and that nature shows no known machinery for restoring the energy which she dissipates. If the physiologists insist on this concession, the Darwinian may perhaps, by way of reaching an issue, content himself with allowing it, with only a single, but serious, restriction.

This single restriction concerns the limitations of science itself, which has thus far penetrated only the grosser operations of nature, and cannot deny that further knowledge may — and probably will — overthrow much of the experience of physics. This possibility is constantly discussed by the most eminent physicists, and is open to endless discussion by physiologists; but since it is the last ground on which the Darwinian can make a stand, he will do well to reserve it, on the chance that new scientific horizons will open to him.

Supposing, then, that the physicist takes the lead, and seeks for a means of compromise, — some middle term, on which the elevationist can stand while discussing the details of a treaty! The degradationist can produce from his stores of energy a number of figures for choice; — such as that of water, which expands or contracts, according to the temperature, or falls according to its position; or electricity, which dissipates itself in work; or of dynamite, which does work by explosion; or of gases, which work restlessly without accomplishing anything; or of table-salt, which dissolves mysteriously in water, to help digestion or stimulate appetite; but possibly he may begin with his favorite figure of a gaseous nebula, and may offer to treat primitive humanity as a volume of human molecules of unequal intensities, tending to dissipate energy, and to correct the loss by concentrating mankind into a single, dense mass like the sun. History would then become a record of successive phases of contraction, divided by periods of explosion, tending always towards an ultimate equilibrium in the form of a volume of human molecules of equal intensity, without coördination.

If this analogy, with its law of phases, should be rejected, the physicist might still offer a number of others, likening social energy to light, heat, electricity, or radiating matter; — in short to any form of physical energy, provided it obeyed his second law of thermodynamics, by dissipating itself beyond recovery; but, with the utmost good-will, the evolutionist will find himself much embarrassed to accept any of these offers. If he is to remain evolutionist, — and he has no other motive for existence, — he is forced to assert, as his most modest claim, the concession of two points: — 1. That organic life has the exclusive power of economizing nature's waste. — 2. That man alone enjoys the supernatural power of consciously reversing nature's process, by raising her dissipated energies, including his own, to higher intensities. That is to say, man must possess the exclusive power of reversing the process of extinction inherent in other activities of nature. The mere conservation of energy would not be enough for him, whatever it is for the glow-worm.

The physicist cannot for a moment be expected to grant either of these demands, and is quite likely to be irritated by them even to the point of flatly denying any exclusive privileges to organic life except in its processes. He is capable of going on to question the value of the processes too, especially on the point of economy, and of asserting that organisms are bad economists compared with inorganic matter. He will readily admit that some of the lower forms of life are economists: — the honey-bee, for example; and some caterpillars which store silk, and the coral polyp which stores lime, and so forth; but the vegetables do much better, with their starch and chlorophyl and carbon, while the ocean and the atmosphere do better still by storing heat on an enormous scale, and distributing it where man needs it; many natural minerals store heat and light and electricity, and part with them for man's uses; the earth itself is supposed to be a storehouse of energy; and the sun is admitted to have stored all sorts of energy in almost infinite volume, for no other known, intelligent use than the purposes of man. Further, steel stores elastic energy better than any vegetable life can do it; every molecule stores cohesive energy better than any animal life does it; while all intelligent people are still staring, with stupid bewilderment, at the storage power of an atom of radium. Matter indeed, is energy itself, and its economies first made organic life possible by thus correcting nature's tendency to waste.

Even less can the physicist admit that man alone enjoys the supernatural power of consciously reversing nature's processes, and of restoring her dissipated energies

to their lost intensity.   From the physicist's point of view,
Man, as a conscious and constant, single, natural force,
seems to have no function except that of dissipating or
degrading energy.   Indeed, the evolutionist himself has
complained, and is still complaining in accents which grow
shriller every day, that man does more to dissipate and
waste nature's economies than all the rest of animal or
vegetable life has ever done to save them.   "Already," —
one may hear the physicists aver — "man dissipates
every year all the heat stored in a thousand million tons of
coal which nature herself cannot now replace, and he
does this only in order to convert some ten or fifteen per
cent of it into mechanical energy immediately wasted
on his transient and commonly purposeless objects.
He draws great reservoirs of coal-oil and gas out of the
earth, which he consumes like the coal.   He is digging
out even the peat-bogs in order to consume them as heat.
He has largely deforested the planet, and hastened its
desiccation.   He seizes all the zinc and whatever other
minerals he can burn, or which he can convert into other
forms of energy, and dissipate into space.   His con-
sumption of oxygen would be proportionate to his waste of
heat, and, according to Kelvin, 'If we burn up our fuel
supplies so fast, the oxygen of the air may become exhausted, and that exhaustion might come about in four

or five centuries' (Life, 1002). He startles and shocks even himself, in his rational moments, by his extravagance, as in his armies and armaments which are made avowedly for no other purpose than to dissipate or degrade energy, or annihilate it as in the destruction of life, on a scale that rivals operations of nature. What is still more curious, his chief pleasures, so far as they are his own invention, consist in gratifying the same unintelligent passion for dissipating or degrading energy, as in drinking alcohol, or burning fireworks, or firing cannon, or illuminating cities, or deafening them by senseless noises. Worse than all, such is his instinct of destruction that he systematically exterminates or degrades all the larger forms of animal life in which nature stored her last creative efforts, while he breeds artificially, at great expense of his own energies, and at cost of the phosphorus and lime accumulated by nature's mostly extinct organisms, the feebler forms of animal and vegetable energies needed to make good the prodigious waste of his own. Physicists and physiologists equally complain of these tendencies in man, and a large part of their effort is now devoted to correcting them; but the physicist adds that, compared with this enormous mass of nature's economies which man dissipates every year in rapid progression, the little he captures from the sun, directly or indirectly, as heat-rays, or water-power, or wind-power, is trifling, and the portion that he restores to higher intensities would be insignificant in any case, even if he did not instantly degrade and dissipate it again for some momentary use."

Against this indictment of man's wastefulness, not even Darwin, fond of paradox as he was, would have cared to champion man's defence, and since Darwin wrote, the waste of energy has been doubled again and again. On this point, the evolutionist stands at great disadvantage. Astronomers are given to holding the sun to a sort of moral accountability because it utilizes only about $\frac{1}{2.300.000.000}$ of its heat, — or gravitation, or electricity, or whatever energies it dissipates, — on any known work, and degrades the rest indefinitely in space; but, if their relative resources are taken into account, the sun is, — according to the physicists, — a model economist compared with man. The sun can keep up its expenditure indefinitely, subject to occasional fits of economy; while man is a bottomless sink of waste unparalleled in the cosmos, and can already see the end of the immense economies which his mother Nature stored for his support. Almost all other organisms, especially the lowest, were good economists, and inorganic matter seemed to be perfect. No physicist dares guess within millions of years the date when the carboniferous forests stored their carbon; but it was an affair of to-day compared with the date when steel stored its elasticity, or the magnet its attraction, or uranium its radiation, or the earth its gravitation; yet the chemists seem unconscious that any of the forms of matter actually known to them, unless it be the radiating activities, have lost or are now degrading their energies, while the higher animals have passed, and are still passing, like dreams.

The evolutionist knows all this quite as well as the degradationist, and has never held man's extravagance for a virtue except in a sense of his own, as though he were to adopt the physicist's figure, and say that the enormous fall of potential which he obtained from all this combustion was utilized or converted by him, and reappeared in the intenser form of energy called Thought. Considered as a mode of motion, Thought was far more valuable than Heat or Electricity, and more much easily stored; it was subject to the usual mechanical laws of attraction and inertia; its analogy with Electricity was declared to be close; and its usefulness was the more important because it had been so carefully economized that its full reservoir could be drawn upon, — as in Universities and schools and libraries, — by all the world without limit, like the oxygen of the air.

In literary language, Thought was God; — Energy in

abstract and absolute form; — the ultimate Substance; — *das Ding an sich.* Most philosophy rested on this idea that Thought is the highest or subtlest energy of nature. The sun is an immense energy, but does its work on earth only by expending 2,300,000,000 times more than equivalent energy in space, while Thought does more work without expending any equivalent energy at all. By placing a lens in the path of the sun's rays, it restores to any given intensity the radiation which had been indefinitely diffused. By cheap mechanical instruments it raises or lowers the intensity of the electric current. By slight motions of the hand it sets chemical energies at work without limit; and, what stamps the act as divine, it impresses the result with FORM.

Thus the dispute drifts back again to the middle-ages. The physicist can no more compromise with the evolutionist than Lord Bacon could compromise with the Schools. Galileo could as well admit that Joshua had held up the sun, as Kelvin could admit the power of man to reverse the dissipation of solar energy, and thus to produce a new energy of higher potential, called Thought; yet even if, for the argument's sake, he had done so, the dispute would not have been settled. If Thought were actually a result of transforming other energies into one of a higher potential, it must still be equally subject to

the laws which governed those energies, and could not
be an independent or supernatural force. Turn or twist
the dilemma as they pleased, they returned to it in spite
of themselves, and would do no better if the evolutionist
were to give way, in his turn, and offer the concession he
had refused.

"On reflection," he might say, "I will grant that
thought may radiate its energy away, like electricity and
heat; a figure which, I understand you to say, suits your
law of degradation while leaving me free to prove, if I
can, its power to rise in intensity. Where will this concession bring me out? You admit that the sun maintains
its energy indefinitely by contracting its volume. Are
you willing to admit that Vital Energy, regarded as a
volume or society, might conceivably do the same thing?
and if so, what then?"

To this, the physicist must be supposed to reply, —
however unwillingly, — that nothing would suit him
better than such a concession, — which he had in fact
begin by offering, — but that, in common honesty, he was
bound to regard it as a total surrender of the evolutionist
claims. The mind either was an independent energy,
or it was not. If evolutionists conceded at the outset
that it was not, then the mere figure mattered nothing;
the dispute ended of itself, and the law of thermodynamics

went into operation.   If, on the contrary, the evolutionists meant to insist on independence, they would gain little or nothing by proving a power to prolong life, — animal, vegetable, or physical, — by aggregation or by concentration; they merely changed the numerical value of the variable called Time : —

"No doubt," might a physicist be imagined to continue, "you can, if you like, give to this variable called Time a value approaching infinity, and this is your ordinary loop-hole of escape.   You are welcome to it, as far as concerns us physicists, and we will help you to get it, and stay in it, if you will only leave us in peace without annoying us by your unscientific, ignorant objections which would put a stop to science altogether, if you insist on them.   Yet when we look at it from your point of view, we cannot see what you gain by increasing the element of Time.   You want to increase not Time but Tension. You do not want to preserve society as it is, — and if you did want it, you could not do it; you want to raise the level of its Vital Energy.   Now, we admit that Vital Energy is not mere attraction or cohesion or elasticity, but we say that it is limited by the same laws, and we know little about any of them except their limitations. Of course, the mind can reverse them in action, but so can they reverse each other, and the mind too; as

cohesion reverses gravitation; and a drop of water reverses cohesion; and one degree of heat reverses all. A
watch-spring stores elasticity better than the mind
stores thought. Any chance bit of obsidian or crystal
can set forests afire, without calling itself intelligent. A
fall of one degree in temperature gives form to an icicle,
without claiming to be divine. A summer shower develops
electricity at a tension sufficient to reverse the energy
of as many minds as get in its way, without asserting the
smallest pretension to reverse natural laws. Nature is
full of rival energies; and, — for anything we know, —
may once have been full of hostile energies; but, hostile
or friendly, its infinite variety of Forms, Directions,
Intensities, and Complexities, had taken order, from the
smallest electron and ion to the widest range of stellar
space measured by the most powerful light-ray, going
through every possible form of physical evolution before
man, — or his instinct, — or his reason, — or any other
animal, or vegetable, or organic life, or vital energy, ever
stirred!"

If then the evolutionist, irritated by treatment which
seems a far-off echo of the remarks of the King of Brob-
dingnag to Gulliver nearly two hundred years ago, should
still insist upon his mind being the highest possible
intensity of energy on account of its consciousness, the

degradationist might probably lose his temper and his manners outright, to the point of breaking out : —

"The psychologists have already told you that Consciousness is only a phase in the decline of vital energy ; — a stage of weakening will. We physicists, even less than you Darwinists, deny the intensity of the Will, but we know it to be stronger in the Scarab or the Scorpion, where it is unconscious, than in Monkey or Man, where it is conscious ; while we watch, over and over again, with abject incredulity, the apotheosis of a butterfly or the flowering of an orchid, which reveal to our scientific sense an intensity of vital energy out of all comparison with that of man. We never tire of marvelling at the essence of substance ; — at the energy of the atom or the glow-worm ; but this is the motive behind our whole thermodynamic law.

"The highest intensities of nature, such as produced the atom and the molecule, were precisely the earliest on our scale. Of the vital energies in the order of time we cannot pretend to know much, since all the types seem to have first developed themselves, during a great many millions of years, in water, or underground, in conditions indefinitely varied and altogether unknown ; but the moment an animal appears above-ground, it turns out to be a Silurian Scorpion, a type of the intensest vital energy that ever lived, if one can trust the entomologists. Next, in the Carboniferous, we happen first on a dragon-fly with 'a spread of wing much exceeding two feet' (Dana, 702). Carboniferous insects, like carboniferous forests, suggest intensities indefinitely stronger in creative power than any energies known to be at work to-day. In fact, no creative energies whatever are known to be at work today, unless it be the radiating activities. Mere heat creates nothing. Neither heat nor its absence accounts for any of the problems of vital energy, — neither for the cell, nor the form, nor the movement, nor the consciousness, nor the descent, nor the inheritance, nor the intelligence, of organisms; nor does motion account for direction. No intelligent man now-a-days is satisfied with a purely mechanical formula.

"Palaeontologists talk only of specialization, as though the more elaborate type were the higher intensity. The opposite is more likely to be true. Geology suggests plainly that, after at least fifty million years of conditions which made life impossible except under water, these anarchic forces dissipated themselves so far as to settle into an equilibrium which showed itself on land in the wild exuberance of the carboniferous forests, and which then developed into the wilder exuberance of the Eocene mammals. How long this exuberance lasted, Saporta

Q

has told us; and he is also authority for the fact, — not the theory, I say, — that the equilibrium was over-thrown by the steady dissipation of energy. Gaudry, another sufficient authority, has added that vital energy fell step by step, and phase by phase, with solar energy. The geologists in general seem to agree with the astronomers in teaching that both forms of energy will continue to fall in intensity until both disappear. Meanwhile we are perfectly at liberty to teach that the relative intensity of each phase measured the relative intensity of each creation of land-organisms in the order of time. We are not only at liberty to do it; we are logically compelled to insist upon it. No other order of sequence can be made to accord with the positively miraculous properties which defy explanation in organic as in inorganic nature.

"We all remember the desperate efforts that Darwin made to fit within a uniformitarian schedule these violent leaps in the energy of evolution, but we seldom realize how difficult he found the task of convincing himself that his own scheme was convenient. When he said, as he often did, that he never thought of the eye without a chill,— 'the eye, to this day (1860), gives me a cold shudder,' — he meant, — among other things, — that his theory was good for nothing as a convenient means of explaining why the eye should have leaped to perfection from its start, when it should have been the slowest in the order of evolution. In fact, the eye of the first fish, at the beginning of geological time, was at least as good as that of his descendant still living unchanged; and the first trilobites, somewhere in Silurian ages, had eyes of twelve or fifteen thousand facets. 'Assuredly,' says Gaudry, 'we marvel at such complication in creatures of such great antiquity, but we cannot conclude that the organ of sight reached its whole perfection in the primary period, for probably the thirty thousand facets of *Remopleurides* were not equal in value to the two beautiful eyes of our actual mammals.' Such a *probably* might well cause Darwin a chill; but had he gone on to say that the decline of the Tertiary quadrupeds caused him a worse shudder, he would have said only what Dana seemed to feel, and what strikes every physicist with astonishment when he reads it in Dana, about the universal stunting of animal life in recent times. In South America alone, during and since the glacial epoch, the extinct species of quadrupeds number more than a hundred, while, among the peculiarly South American order of Ant-eaters, the extinct species were more numerous than all those that 'now exist in that part of the continent, and were far larger animals.' In Australia the Marsupials prove the same law: 'As on the other continents, the moderns are dwarfs by the side of the ancient species.' As a universal rule, the fact of dwindling size holds true of a large part of the mammals, including elephants and herbivores as well as many carnivores, edentates, rodents and marsupials : 'The kinds that continued into modern time became dwindled in the change wherever found over the globe, notwithstanding the fact that genial climates are still to be found over large regions' (Dana, 997). Neither Kelvin nor Faye, neither Lapparent nor Flammarion, asserted the brutal facts of degradation nearly so strongly as Dana.

"To this law, which has already reduced us to 'living in an impoverished world,' you evolutionists require us physicists, under some mysterious penalty, to make for you an exception in favor of man. We cannot do it. We are willing to yield much of the old mechanical ground. We grant that we cannot explain why, in man or in molecule, the primitive energies of nature took directions which imply, — in our limited experience, — a reasoning forethought. Cause is a transcendental problem beyond our grasp. We no longer venture even to assert that we know the creative forces at all. We say only that in the world which we do know, we can see nothing supernatural in action. Infinite complication we admit, but no ultimate contradiction. Sooner or later, every apparent exception, whether man or radium, tends to fall within the domain of physics. Against this necessity, human beings have always rebelled. For thousands of years they have stood apart, superior to physical laws. The time has come when they must yield.

"The claim that Reason must be classed as an energy of the highest intensity is itself unreasonable. On the contrary, Reason is the last in time, and therefore the lowest in tension. According to our western standards, the most intense phase of human Energy occurred in the form of religious and artistic emotion, — perhaps in the Crusades and Gothic Churches; — but since then, though vastly increased in apparent mass, human energy has lost intensity and continues to lose it with accelerated rapidity, as the Church proves. Organized in society, as a volume, it becomes a multiplied number of enfeebled units, on which, like the eye in insects, reason acts as an enormously multiplied lens, converging nature's lines of will, and taking direction from them, but adding nothing of its own. Man has, indeed, — or had, — in a few of his stems, some faculty for artistic expression, not nearly so strong as that of some plants, or some butterflies, or some birds, but more varied. This instinct he probably inherited from an earlier, more gifted, animal;

but as a creative energy he inherited next to nothing.
The coral polyp is a giant beside him.   As an energy he
has but one dominant function : — that of accelerating
the operation of the second law of thermodynamics.   So
far as his reason acts as an energy at all, it is a miraculous
invention for this purpose, which inspires wonder and
almost worship, but in strictness and reason does not
work, — it is only a mechanism; — nature's energy,
which we have agreed to call Will, that lies behind reason,
does the work, — and degrades the energy in doing it !''

Evidently, on these lines, no sort of agreement is
possible.   The two figures contradict each other beyond
the chance of conciliation.   Of course the contradiction
has been slightly exaggerated to make it clear ; but if the
physicist had not himself lost the high literary potential of
Swift and Voltaire, he would exaggerate to much better
purpose, and would handle the unfortunate creature
called Man in a temper such as any one may renew who
cares to go back to Bunyan or Dante or the Bible, not to
mention the Prophets in particular ; but he would convince no one.   Man refuses to be degraded in self-esteem,
of which he has never had enough to save him from bitter
self-reproaches.   He yearns for flattery, and he needs it.
The contradiction between science and instinct is so radical that, though science should prove twenty times over,

by every method of demonstration known to it, that man is a thermodynamic mechanism, instinct would reject the proof, and whenever it should be convinced, it would have to die.

If the deadlock were a new thing, the situation would not be so difficult, but the history of the last five hundred years tells of little else. Man began by usurping the rank of lord of creation. Galileo and Newton succeeded in deposing him, much against his will, — as the Church very candidly confessed, — but he has never despaired of reinstating himself by means of his Reason. The doctrine of evolution seemed, in the nineteenth century, to favor him. For fifty years, society flattered itself that science stood solidly behind it, lifting it up from lower powers to higher, and restoring it to its old rank and self-respect as child and heir to the infinite. The contrary assertion of Kelvin had no effect upon it whatever. Indeed if Eduard von Hartmann is right, society deliberately chose to be silent about the direction of physics, and refused to think or talk about it; but silence has never stopped this dispute, at least in western civilization, since the martyrdom of Prometheus, and merely hurried the moment when, on scientific principles, another catastrophe, like that of the Newtonian philosophy, became imminent.

William Thomson and Clausius, Helmholz and Balfour

Stewart, asserted and reiterated the certainty of this catastrophe, in vain, as Descartes had asserted it, — also in vain, — two hundred years before; but Descartes offered a compromise, and in that respect differed from Kelvin. Descartes proposed to free man from material bondage, provided he might mechanize all other vital energies. Society rose in arms to protect the dog, and so defeated the scheme, leaving the world to go on asserting two contradictory principles in the same breath, down to the present day, to the undiminished embarrassment of Universities, and with little perceptible change in the situation, except that the Universities of to-day hesitate to assert with confidence the old conviction of spiritual authority, showing in this respect a distinct decline in energy; while technical instruction has reached, — or seems on the verge of reaching, — the point where it must insist on the universal application of its thermo-dynamic law.

Since compromise of principle seems to be out of the question, there remains only the resource of direct conflict. Each party is thrown back on the horns of a dilemma, — the same old dilemma of Saint Augustine and Descartes, — the deadlock of free-will. The professor of physics will ask his colleague, the professor of history, to explain the process by which energy raises its own potential without cost, since this has been an object greatly desired by schoolmasters from the earliest known ages, and would singularly simplify the professorial accounts. The teacher of history, who has trouble enough already in trying to raise the potential of his scholars' energy, can only retort by asking his colleague to show how his own teaching proves progressive enfeeblement and degradation of quality. The degradationist might be quite ready to admit it, and quite competent to prove it, but he knows that he has already turned his own thermodynamic law into a means of convincing society of the contrary. Since the year 1830, when the great development of physical energies began, all school-teaching has learned to take for granted that man's progress in mental energy is measured by his capture of physical forces, amounting to some fifty million steam horse-power from coal, and at least as much more from chemical and elementary sources; besides indefinite potentials in his stored experience, and progressive rise in the intensities of the forces he keeps in constant use. He cares little what becomes of all this new power; he is satisfied to know that he habitually develops heat at 3000° Centigrade and electricity by the hundred thousand volts, from sources of indefinitely degraded energy; and that his mind has learned to control them. Man's

Reason once credited with this addition of volume and intensity, its victory seems assured. The teacher of history need then trouble himself with no further doubts of Evolution; but the teacher of physics seems — at least to an ignorant world whose destiny hangs on the balance, — very much required to defend himself.

Although this form of physical psychology is less than a hundred years old it has already taken possession of society so completely as to serve it, in place of the old religious and mechanical formulas, for a philosophical foundation. The historian has a right to use it as such; but according to the understanding of the physical law already discussed, one would think physicists debarred from admitting it. To them it should seem an illusion, although one difficult to deal with; but, as far as a by-stander has means of judging, they would still be at liberty to turn the dilemma about, and seek to impale their antagonist on the reversed horn, by suggesting that the theory of tropism or induction, or of physico-chemical relations in general, seems to require that the psychical will, under such conditions, should not absorb physical energy so much as physical energy would absorb the psychical will. Two similar energies, when in contact, would tend to a common level; force, if powerful enough, would control thought; the ocean would dissolve the crystal of salt; so that, if the evolutionist should insist on identifying the quality of his psychical energy with the quantity of his steam- or water-power or electric voltage, the physicist would expect to see the psychical potential of society vanish as suddenly as the potential of a Leyden jar.

Perhaps the Universities might be quicker than the technical schools to see the point of this retort, since they claim, in theory, to deal with quality rather than with quantity, and possibly some professors have noticed that quality may sometimes suffer from contact with volume. The idea is not precisely new, — far from it ! — even beyond the pale of European Universities, portions of society have shown a somewhat enfeebled instinct of revolt against the psychical processes of the press and the public. Various writers have discussed the effect of dissolving society into a single mixture; even a name, — panmixia — has been made for it. Nothing is commoner than the prejudice against mechanical energy as a weakener of nervous energy whenever it gets control, as in manufacturing towns; or the belief that great masses of people under uniform conditions tend to a mechanical uniformity of mind, as in agricultural districts; but the interest of the subject lies less in the application of the theory than in the shape which the theory would have to take in order to conform with the rest of the law of thermodynamics. Physicists know best what their mathematical formulas for electricity and gases and solutions are; historians have no right to meddle with the methods of colleagues in rival departments; but they cannot help feeling curiosity to know whether Ostwald's line of reasoning would logically end in subjecting both psychical and physico-chemical energies to the natural and obvious analogy of heat, and extending the law of Entropy over all. (Ostwald, "Vorlesungen," Leipzig, 1902, p. 398.)

Few physicists would be likely to see any scientific sense in this personal application of their law, and no one is readier than the historian to admit that vital Energy is probably not so simple as any formula that he could state, or understand if stated to him. The most ardent lover of paradox, — the most inveterate humorist, — would hardly think it worth his while to follow a train of reasoning which would surely immolate physics and metaphysics together. Such amusements seem to be reserved for astronomers; but neither historians nor sociologists can afford to let themselves be driven into admitting that every gain of power, — from gunpowder to steam, — from the dynamo to the Daimler motor, — has been made at the cost of man's — and of woman's — vitality. The mischiefs thus charged upon Reason would not end there. Metaphysics as well as mathematics would measure enfeeblement; philosophy as well as mechanics would mark degradation; the Universities as well as the technical schools would alike close their doors without waiting for the sun to grow cold.

Direct conflict, therefore, seems to be as barren as compromise. Heretofore in human experience, such reasoning would have been dismissed at once as only the usual futile attempt at reduction to the absurd. That it would pass for such in a University of to-day is an open question; it sounds rather like another way of saying what Arndt, Branco, and Hopf, as well as Rousseau and a thousand others have said for the past hundred and fifty years; but in any case it has no value for teachers, since it leads only to the stoppage of teaching altogether. If the teacher of history cares to contest the ground with the teacher of physics, he must become a physicist himself, and learn to use laboratory methods. He needs technical tools quite as much as the electrician does; large formulas, like Willard Gibbs' Rule of Phases; generalizations, no matter how temporary or hypothetical, such as all mathematicians use for the convenience of their scholars. The whole field of physics is covered with such temporary structures, mere approximations to truth, but in constant demand as tools. Mathematicians practise absolute freedom; they have the right — and use it — to assume that a straight line is, or is not, the shortest distance between two points, as they please. In the whole domain of science, no field of cultivation is poorer in such labor-saving devices than that of human history, yet Man, as a form of energy, is in most need of getting a firm footing on the law of thermodynamics. One cannot doubt that Lord Kelvin could have suggested half-a-dozen figures which would answer the purpose, although he might very well have refused to waste his own stock of vital energy in the effort to prove his thermodynamic ascent from a hypothetical eocene lemur, or even from a duck-billed platypus; neither of which would have promised energetic means of saving him from the pitfalls which his keen mathematical instinct would have shown him as the work of his fellow-physicists, planted directly in his path.

Whatever the difficulties, Kelvin would have faced them honestly. He had courage beyond the common, and if the problem had been forced on him as he forced it on others, he would not even have felt himself obliged to obey his own laws. Almost in his last words he pathetically proclaimed that his life was a failure in its long effort to reduce his physical energies to a single term.

Dying he left the unity, duality, or multiplicity of energies as much disputed as ever. "A certain anarchy reigns in the sciences of nature's domain," says M. Lucien Poincaré, who is regarded as a sufficient authority; "any venture may be risked; no law appears rigorously necessary." Within the past year Professor Joly of Dublin has seriously risked such a venture in his "Radio-activity and Geology; an account of the Influence of Radio-active Energy on Terrestrial History" (London, 1909); and although the general reader gathers from it mainly the conclusion that physical science is more or less chaotic, this conclusion is only what he needs to reach before he can begin to deal with vital science, which is all chaos. "We see the middle- and the end-series of the phylogenetic series," says Reinke; "that we do not see the beginning is self-evident, since it was built up in a period of the earth's history which is for us tran-scendental" ("Einleitung," p. 612); we could not understand it if we did see it. So far as concerns the history of man, every period of the earth's history, beyond its actual condition, is transcendental. The anthropologist knows nothing whatever about it. Among a thousand possible varieties of primitive man, he has scarcely more than two or three doubtful clues to follow, and thus far these lead nowhere.

The single point about which Professor Klaatsch speaks with positiveness approaching temper, is that "the primitive man must not be treated either as morally bad or as intellectually stupid. . . . The primitive man, our ancestor, is to be prized as a being high in rank, who, in many a point of view, in force of individuality and vigor of self-assertion (Kraft der Individualität und Kampfesmut) was the superior of his cultured heirs (seinen Epigonen der Kultur)." (Köbner Versammlung der Deutschen Naturforscher und Ärzte. Herbst, 1908.) Apparently this is the only certain result of sixty years' effort in physics and physiology. Forced back on the logical suicide of asserting or accepting an act of creation, biologists prefer to admit mental enfeeblement, even at the risk of being driven to admit both; so that, if the safety of society should seem now to depend on assuming a multiple cause, as of old on establishing the unity of creation, nothing obliges society to persist in its monist scheme. If the physicist cannot make mind the master, as the metaphysician would like, he can at least abstain from making it the slave.

So little essential is monism, that M. H. Poincaré lately startled the world by avowing that physicists used that formula only because all science would become impossible if they were not allowed to assume simple hypotheses ("La Science et l'Hypothèse," p. 173); but this mental need of unity is also a weakness, which gives the degradationist an artificial and altogether unfair advantage. The convenience of unity is beyond question, and convenience overrides morals as well as money, when a vast majority of minds, educated or not, are invited to live in a complex of anarchical energies, with only the privilege of acting as chief anarchists. Bewildered and outraged they reject the image; but they find that of diffusion or degradation so simple and so natural as to satisfy every want. The Darwinian readily admits that Kelvin's sun accounts for evolution better than Darwin's did; and he is only too ready to drop all the school-phrases, — to call the process Transformation, and so, quietly, surrender the issue. He is equally ready to admit that Darwin never supplied a motive power that should vary in force with the phenomena; he might even go so far as to concede that the want of such an energy had embarrassed biology nearly to the point of paralysis; while he must honestly grant that Kelvin began mathematically by giving himself, from the start, all the power he needed, in the degree in which he needed it, so that his system supplied its own force, — like the Niagara River, — by degrading its own energies. Simplicity may not be evidence of truth, and unity is perhaps

R

the most deceptive of all the innumerable illusions of
mind; but both are primary instincts in man, and have
an attraction on the mind akin to that of gravitation
on matter. The idea of unity survives the idea of God
or of Universe; it is innate and intuitive. Thought
floats much more easily towards than against it, and
from the moment when heat, or electricity, or thought,
or any other form or symbol or medium of energy, was
likened to a falling substance tending to an ultimate
ocean of Entropy, nothing was simpler than to plot out
the ordinates and abscissas that marked its curve of
evolution. Astronomy, geology, palaeontology, biology,
psychology, could all move majestically down the decline.

Perhaps the feature of the scheme that was most re-
pulsive to instinct, was most seductive to science, — its
fatal facility in accounting for Reason. All organisms
would tend to develop nervous systems when dynamically
ill-nourished. As the Drosera is represented to have
taken to a diet of insects when it could no longer nourish
itself sufficiently as a vegetable, or as a tree may throw
out wider and deeper roots in the degree that complexity
might bring moisture, so the vital energy which had
developed in the exuberance of physical quantity so long
as its dynamic supplies were in excess of its needs, would
turn itself, as its conditions were impoverished, into those

"connecting, or, as they are technically called, association-fibres, which make nerve-currents work together as they could not without being thus associated." Thought then appears in nature as an arrested, — in other words, as a degraded, — physical action. The theory is convenient, and convenience makes law, at least in the laboratory.

In this freedom of handling his energies the physicist enjoys another easy advantage over the sociologist. As already pointed out, the physicist is safe from interference so long as he can still promise expansion of power, or relief from pain; while the oldest and driest professor of history would smile at the idea of trying to imitate his vivacious colleague by telling his students, at the opening of the collegiate year, that, "as an approximately correct working hypothesis," he should proceed to treat the history of modern Europe and America as a typical example of energies indicating degradation "with head-long rapidity" towards "inevitable death." Probably he would have no more difficulty than the physicist has, in making his material fit his figure; history can be written in one sense just as easily as in another; but however perfect this figure might seem to him he would not think it suited to the interests of the students or of the University, in spite of the fact that the University has never committed itself to the contrary. Indeed he could truthfully say that the Universities in Europe have never preached upward evolution at all.

History began with admitting as its starting-point that the speechless animal who raised himself to the use of an inflected language must have made an effort greater and longer than the effort required for him, after perfecting his tongue, to vulgarize and degrade it. Even after descending to the familiar facts of relatively recent evolution historians never teach that Egyptian pyramids and tombs show childlike inferiority to the tombs and temples of Berlin. Artists have never been known to illustrate their lectures on the history of their art by showing how much the sculpture of Pheidias and Praxiteles might have been improved by an acquaintance with the sculpture of London. Dramatists do not hold up to derision the feebleness of Aeschylus or the folly of Aristophanes before the gigantic force and genius of Sardou and Rostand on the Paris stage. American professors do not read Pindar or Lucretius aloud in order to suit the intelligence of their children in the nurseries of New York and Chicago. Historians seldom express contempt for Thucydides, and still devote volumes to Alexander the Great and Julius Caesar. They have obstinately shirked the duty of applying the law of elevation to their view of history, but rather have bitterly opposed it. Even the prophet of progress in the English school, — Macaulay, — could not resist the old trick of reviving a conventional barbarian to gloat, "in the midst of a vast solitude," — over the exhausted energies of England. Histories invariably use Kelvin's figure whenever it is convenient, and talk of new races in set terms as so much fresh fuel, or oxygen, flung on the burnt-out energies of empire; while the greatest historical work in the English language is called "The Decline and Fall."

Something less than two hundred and fifty years ago, all the greatest scholars and wits of Europe were disputing the relative superiority of ancients and moderns. Swift's "Battle of the Books" still lives as a sparkling record of it. The moderns, having the advantage of being alive, decided the result in their own favor, but, until the amazing influx of mechanical and physical energies after 1830, the European Universities never seemed clear on the subject, and would be quite likely to-day to reverse the judgment on such evidence as decided the case in 1700. Only an unusually well-informed scholar could say with certainty what the German or French Universities think about the dogma of upward evolution in the year 1910, but their record is a bad one.

On the dogma of Degradation their record is worse. If the human race is to depend on their suffrages, its state is a parlous one. For a thousand years, as long as religion held sway, teachers were not merely permitted — they were obliged — to condemn the human race, — with rare exceptions, due only to the pity of God, — to eternal degradation following the near end of the world. After 1500 the Church very slowly lost its control of education, but the attitude of the schools changed little in regard to human history. In the University as in the pulpit, the standard of excellence remained among the Greeks, or the Romans, or the Jews, when it was not carried back to the Garden of Eden. In the nineteenth century, every one knows how eagerly the public responded to Wagner's resuscitation of the Middle Ages. By most artists modern life is assumed as decadence. What is most striking of all, the Universities have begun again, — within fifty years, — to announce through their astronomers the approaching demise of the solar system; through their geologists, the death of the earth and its occupants; through their physicists, the years still left for suns to shine, and the ultimate destiny of the celestial universe to become atomic dust at $-270°$ Centigrade; while their anthropologists point out the rapid exhaustion of the race, and their newspapers day by day proclaim its steady degradation. What makes the matter infinitely worse is the common, daily experience that, not only in Uni-

versities but also at every street-corner of every European
city, on every half-holiday, hundreds of thousands of
men are taught to believe with delight, that society, down
to the present day, is an unnatural abortion, sustained
by perverted illusions, and destined to immediate suicide.
To such a point has this habit of teaching gone, that
society itself, at every national and municipal election,
is seen physically trembling; perplexed and confused;
feeling its way; conscious of its dangers; anxious to do
right; ashamed of the sores which, — as it is solemnly
assured, — disfigure its surface, and of the hideous tumors
which, — as it is incessantly told, — are ravaging its
vitals; half-willing to be sacrificed, like Iphigenia, but
timidly shrinking from staking the life, described as so
worthless, on the gambler's chance of winning something
less wretched in an unknown beyond.

Among all these voluble prophets, the historian alone
may not discuss the problem for respect of youth, lest he
should make still more serious an issue which was serious
before schools began.

If the silent, half-conscious, intuitive faith of society
could be fixed, it might possibly be found always tending
towards belief in a future equilibrium of some sort, that
should end in becoming stable; an idea which belongs
to mechanics, and was probably the first idea that nature

taught to a stone, or to an apple; to a lemur or an ape; before teaching it to Newton. Unfortunately for society, the physicists again abruptly interfere, like Sancho Panza's doctor, by earnest protests that, if one physical law exists more absolute than another, it is the law that stable equilibrium is death. A society in stable equilibrium is — by definition — one that has no history and wants no historians. Thomson and Clausius startled the world by announcing this principle in 1852; but the ants and bees had announced it some millions of years before, as a law of organisms, and it may have been established still earlier, in more convincing form, by some of the caterpillars. According to the recent doctrine of Will or Intuition, this conclusion was the first logical and ultimate result reached in the evolution of organic life; but the professor of history who shall accept the hymenoptera and lepidoptera as teachers in the place of Kelvin and Clausius, will probably find himself in the same dilemma as before. If he aims at carrying his audience with him, he will have to adopt the current view of a society rising to an infinitely high potential of energy, and there remaining in equilibrium, the only view which will insure him the sympathy of men, as well as — probably — of caterpillars; but if he wants to conciliate science, he will have to deride the idea of a stable equilibrium of high potential, and insist that no stable social equilibrium can be reached except by degrading social energies to a level where they can fall no further, and do no more useful work. Perhaps this formula, too, may please many students, whose potential of vital energy, — or, in simpler words, whose love of work, — is less archaic than that of the ants and bees; but as a matter of practical teaching, — as a mere choice between technical formulas, — the two methods result in the same dilemma for the old-fashioned evolutionist who clings to his ideals of indefinite progress. Between two equilibriums, each mechanical, and each insisting that history is at an end, lost forever in the ocean of statistics, the classical University teacher of history, with his intuitions of free-will and art, can exist only as a sporadic survival to illustrate for his colleagues the workings of their second law of thermodynamics.

To some extent, already, he finds himself actually in this awkward situation where his colleagues betray impatience at his continued existence. With singular unanimity, the polite, but embarrassed authorities agree that history is not a science, and show marked unwillingness to permit that it shall ever, with their consent, become one. Except on their own terms, they will have nothing to do with human evolution, and their terms commonly require that they should treat man as a creature habitually striving to attain imaginary ideals always contrary to law. His Will and that of Nature have been constantly at strife, and continue to be so, under the Baconian philosophy and the law of *Energetik*, as decidedly as under the scholastic philosophy and the Summa of St. Thomas Aquinas. Even the friendly Vitalist treats his brother Vitalists with candor not to be mistaken for compliment, because, "in the history of humanity there is always only so much science as there is *no* History"; while the most *naïf* of all the historian's *naïvetés* is his favorite notion that the "understanding" of a problematic humanity can be furthered by adding to it a more problematic phantom of Descent. (Driesch, "Naturbegriffe und Natururtheile." Leipzig, 1904, p. 237.) In truth, one is driven to admit that "the theory of descent," as Von Zittel says, "has introduced new ideas into descriptive natural history, and has given it a higher purpose; but we must not forget that it is still only a theory, which requires to be proved."

On this point, the professor of history who has any smattering of special training, knows all that he needs to know. He is as free as ever he was to go on compiling tables of dates, or editing, or reëditing so-called "documents," or seeking to infuse into the memories of his

students a sufficient acquaintance with the statute Quia
Emptores. He has fully made up his mind either for
or against the existence of any philosophy at all, as well
as whether he is required to lecture on such a philosophy
in case it does, or does not, exist. Every competent
teacher of history is supposed, justly or unjustly, to know
his Herbert Spencer and Auguste Comte, even if not his
Lamprecht. When his physiological colleagues ridicule
his aspirations to science, the professor of history seems
little disposed to resent their attitude, but rather en-
courages it; and he is right, if they are right, in doing
so; but, none the less, he finds himself thus placed, for
the first time in three hundred years, face to face with a
painful, if not a vital problem. In one respect his dilemma
is worse than in the sixteenth century, since Bacon's
physical teaching aimed at freeing the mind from a
servitude, while the law of Entropy imposes a servitude
on all energies, including the mental. The degree of
freedom steadily and rapidly diminishes. Without rest,
the physicists gently push history down the decline, as
yet scarcely conscious, which they are certain to plot
out by abscissae and ordinates as soon as they can fix
and agree upon a sufficient number of normal variables,
not with conscious intention but by unconscious extension.
Every reader of current literature knows that the subject

is touched by half the books he reads, and that the most popular are the most outspoken. Few volumes are more widely known than M. Gustave Le Bon's "Physiologie des Foules" (1895), which closes with the following paragraph : —

"That which formed a people, a unity, a block, ends by becoming an agglomeration of individuals without cohesion, still held together for a time by its traditions and institutions. This is the phase when men, divided by their interests and aspirations, but no longer knowing how to govern themselves, ask to be directed in their smallest acts ; and when the State exercises its absorbing influence. With the definitive loss of the old ideal, the race ends by entirely losing its soul ; it becomes nothing more than a dust of isolated individuals, and returns to what it was at the start, — a crowd."

Under the thinnest veil of analogy the physicist-historian, with scientific calmness, condemns our actual society as he condemns the sun ; for the "crowd" which Gustave Le Bon declares to be the end of social evolution is not at all the same "crowd" that made its beginning, and is wholly incapable of doing useful work. In the very teeth of his own arguments and aims Gustave Le Bon in his last volume, "La Psychologie Politique" (Paris, 1910), affirms that this process has already reached its critical point : —

"The surest symptom of the decadence threatening us is the general enfeeblement of characters. Numerous to-day are the men whose energy weakens, especially among the choicest, who should be precisely those who need it most, with the great masters who are placed at the head of nations, as well as with the small chiefs who govern in details, indecision and weakness become dominant. . . . Among the forces of which man disposes, in order to struggle successfully against the powers which constrain him, the Will was always the most active. . . . If we try then to discover why so many nations perished after a long decline, — why Rome formerly queen of the world, ended by falling under the barbarian's yoke, we find that these profound falls had generally the same cause, — enfeeblement of the Will" (pp. 374-5). "It was always by this enfeeblement of character, and not by that of intelligence that the great peoples disappeared from history" (p. 295). "It would even seem as though to-day the dead alone gave us energy" (p. 372). This is the teaching of a physicist, but the medical authorities on psychic disease are even more outspoken, frankly asserting as a fact, on which their teaching rests, that the weakness of the Will is the great malady of our epoch. (Grasset, "Idées Medicales." Paris, 1910, p. 56.) Among these medical experts, Dr.

Forbes Winslow in his "Recollections" has scandalized the community by his bluntness : — "On comparing the human race during the past forty years," he says (pp. 376–377), "I have no hesitation in stating that it has degenerated, and is still progressing in a downward direction. We are gradually approaching, with the decadence of youth, a near proximity to a nation of madmen. By comparing the lunacy statistics of 1809 with those of 1909, . . . an insane world is looked forward to by me with a certainty in the not far distant future." In fact, the statistics show that in 1809 there was one lunatic in every 418 of the total population of England and Wales ; in 1909, there was one in every 278 ; so that in three hundred years one half the population should be insane or idiotic. "These are facts !" continues Dr. Forbes Winslow ; "they cannot in any way be challenged."

Gustave Le Bon is himself a physicist of wide renown, but he is remarkable also as director of the "Bibliothèque de Philosophie Scientifique," the best known of all recent attempts to lighten the load of technical instruction and of scientific baggage. Among the most recent of these admirable volumes is one on "Degradation" (Paris, November, 1908), by M. Bernhard Brunhes, whose position as Director of the Observatory of the Puy de Dôme guarantees his competence to narrate the story.

In one or two paragraphs, with the lucidity which so often distinguishes French thought from that of some other races, M. Brunhes summarizes the values of the two philosophies of history : —

"The preceding remarks give the key to the apparent opposition which exists between the doctrine of Evolution and the principle of Degradation of energy. Physical science presents to us a world which is unceasingly wearing itself out. A philosophy which claims to derive support from biology, paints complacently, on the contrary, a world steadily improving, in which physiological life goes on always growing perfect to the point of reaching full consciousness of itself in man, and where no limit seems imposed on eternal progress. Observe that this second idea, — of indefinite progress, — has furnished much more material than the first, for literary development! This is no doubt because the scientific facts on which it is constructed lend themselves to vulgarization far more easily than the scientific facts whose combination forms the principle of Carnot. From our point of view the principle of Degradation of energy would prove nothing against the fact of Evolution. The progressive transformation of species, the realization of more perfect organisms, contain nothing contrary to the idea of the constant loss of useful energy. Only the vast and grandiose conceptions of imaginative philosophers who erect into an absolute principle the law of 'universal progress,' could no longer hold against one of the most fundamental ideas that physics reveals to us. On one side, therefore, the world wears out; on another side the appearance on earth of living beings more and more elevated, and, — in a slightly different order of ideas, — the development of civilization in human society, undoubtedly give the impression of a progress and a gain" (p. 193).

This, then, is the extreme limit of the physicists' concessions. If a compromise is to be made, it must rest there. The degradationist can so far ameliorate the immediate rigor of his law as to admit that degradation of energy may create, or convey, an impression of progress and gain; but if the evolutionist presses the inquiry further, and asks where this proposed compromise will lead him as a teacher of young men, — what future reality lies behind the impression of progress, — what amount of illusion is to be reckoned as an independent variable in the formula of gain, — the degradationist replies, quite candidly and honestly, that this impression of gain is derived from an impression of Order due to the levelling of energies; but that the impression of Order is an illusion consequent on the dissolution of the higher Order which had supplied, by lowering its inequalities, all the useful energies that caused progress. The reality behind the illusion, is, therefore, absence of the power to do useful work, — or what man knows in his finite sensibilities as death : —

"Thus Order in the material universe would be the mark of utility and the measure of value; and this Order, far from being spontaneous, would tend constantly to destroy itself. Yet the Disorder towards which a collection of molecules moves, is in no respect the initial chaos rich in differences and inequalities that generate useful energies; on the contrary it is the average mean of equality and homogeneity in absolute want of coördination" (p. 53).

Perhaps an instructor needs a memory extending over sixty years in order to measure the revolution in thought which such teaching implies. Every right-minded University Professor of 1850 dismissed the ideas of Kelvin as he did those of Malthus, Karl Marx, and Schopenhauer, as fantastic. They shocked him partly for their extravagance but chiefly for what he regarded as their destructive pessimism. In 1910 an American professor who should try to get below the surface of thought in Germany, Italy, France, or even in England, would probably incline to the conclusion that Schopenhauer may be regarded as an optimist. In reality pessimists and op-

s

timists have united on a system of science which makes pessimism the logical foundation of optimism. History is the victim of both. Let any young student take up the last German book on Biology that happens to fall under his eyes. Within the first hundred pages he is fairly sure to come upon some assertion or assumption of the second law of thermodynamics in its dogmatic form : —

"The *Energetik* of the living organism consists, then, in the last analysis, in the fact that the organism, when left to itself, tends in the direction of a stable equilibrium under the surrender of energy to the outer world. The reaching of the stable equilibrium, — even the mere approach to it, — means death. In this respect the organism acts like a clock that has run down." (Reinke, "Einleitung in die theoretische Biologie," p. 152.)

In 1852, Thomson contented himself by saying that a restoration of energy is "probably" never effected by organized matter. In 1910, there is nothing "probable" about it ; the fact has become an axiom of biology. In 1852, any University professor would have answered this quotation by the dry remark that society was not an organism, and that history was not a science, since it could not be treated mathematically. To-day, M. Bernhard Brunhes seems to feel no doubt that society is an organism, and the most marked tendency of recent historians is to reassert in almost dogmatic terms the historical fact that man is the creature, not the creator, of the social organism. Among living historians Eduard Meyer stands near the head, and his introduction begins with the axiom that "the whole mental development of mankind has, for its preliminary assumption, the existence of separate social groups."

"Above all, the weightiest instrument of men, Speech — which first makes the Man, and first makes possible the growth of our systematic Thought, — has not been a casual creation of individuals or of the relation between parents and children, but has grown out of the common needs of equals, bound together by common interests and regulated intercourse. But even the invention of tools, such as the acquisition of Fire, the taming of the domestic Animals, the settlement in Residence, and so on, are possible only within a group; or at least have meaning only so far as what has first and immediately benefited one, becomes the property of the whole community. That, in general, Manners, Law, Religion, and all such moral properties can have arisen only in such relations, needs no discussion. Thus the organization in such ties (Hordes, Stocks) which we meet in experience everywhere we get to know man is not merely just as old, but is far older than the Man; it is the preliminary condition of the existence of the human race altogether." (Einleitung, 7, 8.)

Even the child is the creature of the State Organism, not of the Family. "The generation and bringing up of the descendants lies much nearer the heart of the Social organism than of the individual man, for to him his own life is his chief interest, while to every social group the actual living members are wholly irrelevant in themselves, and only the momentary representatives of the chain of generations. . . . Hence the compulsion to marriage, and the care for the birth and bringing up of a posterity; hence also the decision whether a new-born child shall live and become a member of the society is for the most part not left to choice of the parent, but falls to the kin or to some other recognized public authority" (p. 20). In short, the social Organism, in the recent views of history, is the cause, creator, and end of the Man, who exists only as a passing representative of it, without rights or functions except what it imposes. As an Organism society has always been peculiarly subject to degradation of Energy, and alike the historians and the physicists invariably stretch Kelvin's law over all organized matter whatever. Instead of being a mere convenience in treatment, the law is very rapidly be-

coming a dogma of absolute Truth. As long as the theory
of Degradation, — as of Evolution, — was only one of
the convenient tools of science, the sociologist had no
just cause for complaint. Every science, — and mathematics first of all, — uses what tools it likes. The Professor of Physics is not teaching Ethics; he is training
young men to handle concrete energy in one or more of
its many forms, and he has no choice but to use the most
convenient formulas. Unfortunately the formula most
convenient for him is not at all convenient for his colleagues in sociology and history, without pressing the
inquiry further, into more intimate branches of practice
like medicine, jurisprudence, and politics. If the entire
universe, in every variety of active energy, organic and
inorganic, human or divine, is to be treated as clock-
work that is running down, society can hardly go on ignor-
ing the fact forever. Hitherto it has often happened
that two systems of education, like the Scholastic and
Baconian, could exist side by side for centuries, — as
they exist still, — in adjoining schools and universities,
by no more scientific device than that of shutting their
eyes to each other; but the universe has been terribly
narrowed by thermodynamics. Already History and
Sociology gasp for breath.

The department of history needs to concert with the

departments of biology, sociology, and psychology some common formula or figure to serve their students as a working model for their study of the vital energies; and this figure must be brought into accord with the figures or formulas used by the department of physics and mechanics to serve their students as models for the working of physico-chemical and mechanical energies. Without the adhesion of physicists, the model would cause greater scandal than though the contradictions were silently ignored as now; but the biologists, — or, at least, the branches of science concerned with humanity, — will find great difficulty in agreeing on any formula which does not require from physics the abandonment, in part, of the second law of thermodynamics. The mere formal exception of Reason from the express operation of the law, as a matter of teaching in the workshop, is not enough. Either the law must be abandoned in respect to Vital Energy altogether, or Vital Energy must abandon Reason altogether as one of its forms, and return to the old dilemma of Descartes.

Meanwhile nothing prevents each instructor from aiming to unite with each of his colleagues in some sort of approach to a common understanding about the first principle of instruction; if each University solves the problem to its own satisfaction, the problem is, in so far, solved for the whole; and nothing need hamper the effort of the Universities to carry the process further, if it promises advantage. If the physicists and physico-chemists can at last find their way to an arrangement that would satisfy the sociologists and historians, the problem would be wholly solved. Such a complete solution seems not impossible; but at present, — for the moment, — as the stream runs, — it also seems, to an impartial bystander, to call for the aid of another Newton.

THE RULE OF PHASE APPLIED TO HISTORY

1909

THE RULE OF PHASE APPLIED TO HISTORY

IN 1876–1878 Willard Gibbs, Professor of Mathematical Physics at Yale, published in the Transactions of the Connecticut Academy his famous memoir on the "Equilibrium of Heterogeneous Substances," containing the short chapter "On Existent Phases of Matter," which, in the hands of the Dutch chemists, became, some ten years afterwards, a means of greatly extending the science of Static Chemistry. Although the name of Willard Gibbs is probably to-day the highest in scientific fame of all Americans since Benjamin Franklin, his Rule of Phases defies translation into literary language. The mathematical formulas in which he hid it were with difficulty intelligible to the chemists themselves, and are quite unintelligible to an unmathematical public, while the sense in which the word Phase was used, confused its meaning to a degree that alters its values, and reduces it to a chemical relation. Willard Gibbs helped to change the face of science, but his Phase was not the Phase of History.

As he used it, the word meant Equilibrium, which is in fact the ordinary sense attached to it, but his equilibrium was limited to a few component parts. Ice, water, and water-vapor were three phases of a single substance, under different conditions of temperature and pressure; but if another element were added, — if one took sea-water, for instance, — the number of phases was increased according to the nature of the components. The chemical phase thus became a distinct physical section of a solution, and as many sections existed as there were independent components.

The common idea of phase is that of the solution itself, as when salt is dissolved in water. It is the whole equilibrium or state of apparent rest. It means, perhaps, when used of movement, a variance of direction, but it seems not to have been so much employed to indicate a mere change in speed. Yet the word would apply in literature as well as it does in physical chemistry to the three stages of equilibrium: ice, water, and steam. Where only one component is concerned, the Rule of Phase is the same for chemistry as for general usage. A change of phase, in all cases, means a change of equilibrium.

Whether the equilibrium or phase is temporary or permanent, — whether the change is rapid or slow, — whether the force at work for the purpose is a liquid solvent, or heat, or a physical attraction or repulsion, —

the interest of the equilibrium lies in its relations, and the object of study is the behavior of each group under new relations. Chemists and physicists have turned their studies, for twenty or thirty years past, to these relations, and the various conditions of temperature, pressure, and volume have become more important than the atoms and molecules themselves, while new processes, — osmosis, electrolysis, magnetic action, — have made a new world that is slowly taking the place of the world as it existed fifty years ago; though as yet the old curriculum of thought has been hardly touched by the change.

The new field can be entered only by timid groping for its limits, and with certainty of constant error; but in order to enter it at all, one must begin by following the lines given by physical science. If the Rule of Phase is to serve for clue, the first analogy which imposes itself as the starting-point for experiment is the law of solutions, which seems to lie on the horizon of science as the latest and largest of possible generalizations. As science touches every material or immaterial substance, each in its turn dissolves, until the ether itself becomes an ocean of discontinuous particles.

A solution is defined as a homogeneous mixture, which can pass through continuous variations of composition within the limits that define its existence. Solids, as we all know, may be dissolved, but we do not all realize that liquids and gases may also be dissolved, or that a change in composition must accompany a change of phase. As early as 1662, Isaac Voss, in his work, "De Lucis Natura," on the Nature of Light, defined Heat as "actus dissolvens corpora," the solvent of material bodies; and in 1870, the French chemist Rosenstiehl published a paper in the Comptes Rendues of the French Academy (vol. LXX) suggesting that any gas might be likened to a body dissolved in the medium of the universal solvent, the ether. Reversing the theory, the English and Dutch physicists have solidified every gas, including even helium. The solvent has been suggested or found for every form of matter, even the most subtle, until it trembles on the verge of the ether itself; and a by-stander, who is interested in watching the extension of this new synthesis, cannot help asking himself where it can find a limit. If every solid is soluble into a liquid, and every liquid into a gas, and every gas into corpuscles which vanish in an ocean of ether, — if nothing remains of energy itself except potential motion in absolute space, — where can science stop in the application of this fecund idea?

Where it can stop is its own affair, dependent on its own will or convenience; but where it must stop is a larger question that interests philosophy. There seems to

be no reason for insisting that it must necessarily stop
anywhere within the region of experience. Certainly it
cannot stop with static electricity, which is itself more
obviously a mere phase than water-vapor. The physicists
cannot conceive it without conceiving something more
universal behind or above it. The logic of former
thought, in its classic simplicity, would have taken for
granted that electricity must be capable of reduction to a
solid, — that it can be frozen, — and that it must also
be soluble in ether. One has learned to distrust logic,
and to expect contradiction from nature, but we cannot
easily prevent thought from behaving as though sequence
were probable until the contrary becomes still more
probable; and the mind insists on asking what would
happen if, in the absence of known limit, every substance
that falls within human experience should be soluble
successively in a more volatile substance, or under more
volatile conditions. Supposing the mechanical theories of
matter to be carried out as far as experience warrants, —
supposing each centre of motion capable of solution in a less
condensed motion,—supposing every vortex-centre treated
as a phase or stage of equilibrium which passes, more or
less abruptly, into another phase, under changed conditions; must all motion merge at last into ultimate static
energy existing only as potential force in absolute space?

The reply of the physicist is very simple as a formula of experiment; he can carry his theory no further than he can carry his experience; but how far does he, as a matter of fact, carry his habitual, ordinary experience? Time was when experiment stopped with matter perceptible to the senses; but the chemist long ago lost sight of matter so limited. Vehemently resisting, he had been dragged into regions where supersensual forces alone had play. Very unwillingly, after fifty years of struggle, chemists had been forced to admit the existence of inconceivable and incredible substances, and their convulsive efforts to make these substances appear comprehensible had measured the strain on their thought. Static electricity already lay beyond the legitimate domain of sensual science, while beyond static electricity lay a vast supersensual ocean roughly called the ether which the physicists and chemists, on their old principles, were debarred from entering at all, and had to be dragged into, by Faraday and his school. Beyond the ether, again, lay a vast region, known to them as the only substance which they knew or could know — their own thought,—which they positively refused to touch.

Yet the physicists here, too, were helpless to escape the step, for where they refused to go as experimenters, they had to go as mathematicians. Without the higher mathematics they could no longer move, but with the higher mathematics, metaphysics began. There the restraints of physics did not exist. In the mathematical order, infinity became the invariable field of action, and not only did the mathematician deal habitually and directly with all sorts of infinities, but he also built up hyper-infinites, if he liked, or hyper-spaces, or infinite hierarchies of hyper-space. The true mathematician drew breath only in the hyper-space of Thought; he could exist only by assuming that all phases of material motion merged in the last conceivable phase of immaterial motion — pure mathematical thought.

The physicist, in self-defence, though he may not deny, prefers to ignore this rigorous consequence of his own principles, as he refused for many years to admit the consequences of Faraday's experiments; but at least he can surely rely upon this admission being the last he will ever be called upon to make. No phase of hyper-substance more subtle than thought can ever be conceived, since it could exist only as his own thought returning into itself. Possibly, in the inconceivable domains of abstraction, the ultimate substance may show other sides or extensions, but to man it can be known only as hyper-thought, — the region of pure mathematics and metaphysics, — the last and universal solvent.

There even mathematics must stop. Motion itself

T

ended; even thought became merely potential in this final solution. The hierarchy of phases was complete. Each phase, measured by its rapidity of vibration, arranged itself in the physical sequence familiar to physicists, such as that sketched by Stoney in his well-known memoirs of 1885, 1890, and 1899, and as reasonable as the solar spectrum. The hierarchy rose in an order more or less demonstrable, from : —

1. The *Solids,* among which the Rule of Phases offers ice as a convenient example of its first phase, because under a familiar change of temperature it passes instantly into its next phase : —

2. The *Fluid,* or water, which by a further change of temperature transforms itself suddenly into the third phase : —

3. *Vapor,* or gas, which has laws and habits of its own forming the chief subject of chemical study upon the molecule and the atom. Thus far, each phase falls within the range of human sense, but the gases, under new conditions, seem to resolve themselves into a fourth phase : —

4. The Electron or *Electricity,* which is not within the range of any sense except when set in motion. Another form of the same phase is Magnetism; and some psychologists have tried to bring animal consciousness or thought into relation with electro-magnetism, which

would be very convenient for scientific purposes. The most prolonged and painful effort of the greatest geniuses has not yet succeeded in uniting Electricity with Magnetism, much less with Mind, but all show the strongest signs of a common origin in the next phase of undifferentiated energy or energies called: —

5. The *Ether*, endowed with qualities which are not so much substantial or material as they are concepts of thought, — self-contradictions in experience. Very slowly and unwillingly have the scientists yielded to the necessity of admitting that this form of potential energy — this undifferentiated substance supporting matter and mind alike — exists, but it now forms the foundation of physics, and in it both mind and matter merge. Yet even this semi-sensual, semi-concrete, inconceivable complex of possibilities, the agent or home of infinite and instantaneous motion like gravitation, — infinitely rigid and infinitely elastic at once, — is solid and concrete compared with its following phase: —

6. *Space*, knowable only as a concept of extension, a thought, a mathematical field of speculation, and yet almost the only concrete certainty of man's consciousness. Space can be conceived as a phase of potential strains or disturbances of equilibrium, but whether studied as static substance or substance in motion, it must be endowed with

an infinite possibility of strain. That which is infinitely formless must produce form. That which is only intelligible as a thought, must have a power of self-induction or disturbance that can generate motion.

7. Finally, the last phase conceivable is that which lies beyond motion altogether as Hyper-space, knowable only as Hyper-thought, or pure mathematics, which, whether a subjective idea or an objective theme, is the only phase that man can certainly know and about which he can be sure. Whether he can know it from more than one side, or otherwise than as his own self-consciousness, or whether he can ever reach higher phases by developing higher powers, is a matter for mathematicians to decide; but, even after reducing it to pure negation, it must still possess, in the abstractions of ultimate and infinite equilibrium, the capacity for self-disturbance; it cannot be absolutely dead.

The Rule of Phases lends itself to mathematical treatment, and the rule of science which is best suited to mathematical treatment will always be favored by physicists, other merits being equal. Though the terms be as general as those of Willard Gibbs' formulas, if they hold good for every canonical system they will be adopted. The Rule itself assumes the general fact, ascertained by experiment or arbitrarily taken as starting point, that every equilibrium, or phase, begins and ends with what is called a critical point, at which, under a given change of temperature or pressure, a mutation occurs into another phase; and that this passage from one to the other can always be expressed mathematically. The time required for establishing a new equilibrium varies with the nature or conditions of the substance, and is sometimes very long in the case of solids, but the formula does not vary.

In chemistry the Rule of Phase applied only to material substances, but in physics no such restriction exists. Down to the moment of Hertz's experiments in 1887 and 1888, common-sense vigorously rejected the idea that material substance could be reduced to immaterial energy, but this resistance had to be abandoned with the acceptance of magneto-electricity and ether, both of which were as immaterial as thought itself; and the surrender became final with the discovery of radium, which brought the mutation of matter under the closest direct observation. Thenceforward nothing prevented the mathematical physicist from assuming the existence of as many phases, and calculating the values of as many mutations, as he liked, up to the last thinkable stage of hyperthought and hyperspace which he knew as pure mathematics, and in which all motion, all relation, and all form, were merged.

The laws governing potential strains and stresses in an ideal equilibrium infinitely near perfection, or the volatility of an ideal substance infinitely near a perfect rest, or the possibilities of self-induction in an infinitely attenuated substance, may be left to mathematics for solution; but the ether, with its equally contradictory qualities, is admitted to exist; it is a real substance — or series of substances, — objective and undeniable as a granite rock. It is an equilibrium, a phase, with laws of its own which are not the laws of Newtonian mechanics; it requires new methods, perhaps new mind; but, as yet, the physicist has found no reason to exclude it from the sequence of substances. The dividing line between static electricity and ether is hardly so sharp as that between any of the earlier phases, — solid, fluid, gaseous, or electric.

The physicist has been reluctantly coerced into this concession, and if he had been also a psychologist he would have been equally driven, under the old laws of association formerly known as logic, to admit that what he conceded to motion in its phase as matter, he must concede to motion in its form as mind. Without this extension, any new theory of the universe based on mechanics must be as ill-balanced as the old. Whatever dogmatic confidence the mechanist had professed in his mechanical theory of the universe, his own mind had always betrayed an uneasy protest against being omitted from its own mechanical creation.   This neglect involved not only a total indifference to its claim to exist as a material — or immaterial — vibration, although such mere kinetic movement was granted in theory to every other substance it knew; but it ignored also the higher claim, which was implied in its own definition, that it existed as the sole source of Direction, or Form, without which all mechanical systems must remain forever as chaotic as they show themselves in a thousand nebulae.   The matter of Direction was more vital to science than all kinematics together.   The question how order could have got into the universe at all was the chief object of human thought since thought existed; and order, — to use the expressive figure of Rudolph Goldscheid, — was but Direction regarded as stationary, like a frozen waterfall.   The sum of motion without direction is zero, as in the motion of a kinetic gas where only Clerk Maxwell's demon of Thought could create a value.   Possibly, in the chances of infinite time and space, the law of probabilities might assert that, sooner or later, some volume of kinetic motion must end in the accident of Direction, but no such accident has yet affected the gases, or imposed a general law on the visible universe.   Down to our day Vibration and Direction remain as different as Matter and Mind.   Lines of force go on vibrating, rotating, moving in waves, up and down, forward and back, indifferent to control and pure waste of energy, — forms of repulsion, — until their motion becomes guided by motive, as an electric current is induced by a dynamo.

History, so far as it recounts progress, deals only with such induction or direction, and therefore in history only the attractive or inductive mass, as Thought, helps to construct. Only attractive forces have a positive, permanent value for the advance of society on the path it has actually pursued. The processes of History being irreversible, the action of Pressure can be exerted only in one direction, and therefore the variable called Pressure in physics has its equivalent in the Attraction, which, in the historical rule of phase, gives to human society its forward movement. Thus in the historical formula, Attraction is equivalent to Pressure, and takes its place.

In physics, the second important variable is Temperature. Always a certain temperature must coincide with a certain pressure before the critical point of change in phase can be reached. In history, and possibly wherever the movement is one of translation in a medium, the Temperature is a result of acceleration, or its equivalent, and in the Rule of historical phase Acceleration takes its place.

The third important variable in the physico-chemical phase is Volume, and it reappears in the historical phase unchanged.   Under the Rule of Phase, therefore, man's Thought, considered as a single substance passing through a series of historical phases, is assumed to follow the analogy of water, and to pass from one phase to another through a series of critical points which are determined by the three factors Attraction, Acceleration, and Volume, for each change of equilibrium.   Among the score of figures that might be used to illustrate the idea, that of a current is perhaps the nearest ; but whether the current be conceived as a fluid, a gas, or as electricity, — whether it is drawn on by gravitation or induction, — whether it be governed by the laws of astronomical or electric mass, — it must always be conceived as a solvent, acting like heat or electricity, and increasing in volume by the law of squares.

This solvent, then, — this ultimate motion which absorbs all other forms of motion is an ultimate equilibrium, — this ethereal current of Thought, — is conceived as existing, like ice on a mountain range, and trickling from every pore of rock, in innumerable rills, uniting always into larger channels, and always dissolving whatever it meets, until at last it reaches equilibrium in the ocean of ultimate solution.   Historically the current can be watched for only a brief time, at most ten thousand years. Inferentially it can be divined for perhaps a hundred thousand. Geologically it can be followed back perhaps a hundred million years, but however long the time, the origin of consciousness is lost in the rocks before we can reach more than a fraction of its career.

In this long and — for our purposes — infinite stretch of time, the substance called Thought has, — like the substance called water or gas, — passed through a variety of phases, or changes, or states of equilibrium, with which we are all, more or less, familiar. We live in a world of phases, so much more astonishing than the explosion of rockets, that we cannot, unless we are Gibbs or Watts, stop every moment to ask what becomes of the salt we put in our soup, or the water we boil in our teapot, and we are apt to remain stupidly stolid when a bulb bursts into a tulip, or a worm turns into a butterfly. No phase compares in wonder with the mere fact of our own existence, and this wonder has so completely exhausted the powers of Thought that mankind, except in a few laboratories, has ceased to wonder, or even to think. The Egyptians had infinite reason to bow down before a beetle; we have as much reason as they, for we know no more about it; but we have learned to accept our beetle Phase, and to recognize that everything, animate or inanimate, spiritual or material, exists in Phase; that all is equilibrium more or less unstable, and that our whole vision is limited to the bare possibility of calculating in mathematical form the degree of a given instability.

Thus results the plain assurance that the future of Thought, and therefore of History, lies in the hands of the physicists, and that the future historian must seek his education in the world of mathematical physics. Nothing can be expected from further study on the old lines. A new generation must be brought up to think by new methods, and if our historical department in the Universities cannot enter this next Phase, the physical department will have to assume the task alone.

Meanwhile, though quite without the necessary education, the historical inquirer or experimenter may be permitted to guess for a moment, — merely for the amusement of guessing, — what may perhaps turn out to be a possible term of the problem as the physicist will take it up. He may assume, as his starting-point, that Thought is a historical substance, analogous to an electric current, which has obeyed the laws, — whatever they are, — of Phase. The hypothesis is not extravagant. As a fact, we know only too well that our historical Thought has obeyed, and still obeys, some law of Inertia, since it has habitually and obstinately resisted deflection by new forces or motives; we know even that it acts as though it felt friction from resistance, since it is constantly stopped by all sorts of obstacles; we can apply to it, letter for letter, one of the capital laws of physical chemistry, that, where an equilibrium is subjected to conditions which tend to change, it reacts internally in ways that tend to resist the external constraint, and to preserve its established balance; often it is visibly set in motion by sympathetic forces which act upon it as a magnet acts on soft iron, by induction; the commonest school-history takes for granted that it has shown periods of unquestioned acceleration. If, then, society has in so many ways obeyed the ordinary laws of attraction and inertia, nothing can be more natural than to inquire whether it obeys them in all respects, and whether the rules that have been applied to fluids and gases in general, apply also to society as a current of Thought. Such a speculative inquiry is the source of almost all that is known of magnetism, electricity and ether, and all other possible immaterial substances, but in history the inquiry has the vast advantage that a Law of Phase has been long established for the stages of human thought.

No student of history is so ignorant as not to know that fully fifty years before the chemists took up the study of Phases, Auguste Comte laid down in sufficiently precise terms a law of phase for history which received the warm adhesion of two authorities, — the most eminent of that day, — Émile Littré and John Stuart Mill. Nearly a hundred and fifty years before Willard Gibbs announced his mathematical formulas of phase to the physicists and chemists, Turgot stated the Rule of historical Phase as clearly as Franklin stated the law of electricity. As far as concerns theory, we are not much further advanced now than in 1750, and know little better what electricity or thought is, as substance, than Franklin and Turgot knew it; but this failure to penetrate the ultimate synthesis of nature is no excuse for professors of history to abandon the field which is theirs by prior right, and still less can they plead their ignorance of the training in mathematics and physics which it was their duty to seek. The theory of history is a much easier study than the theory of light.

It was about 1830 that Comte began to teach the law that the human mind, as studied in the current of human thought, had passed through three stages or phases: — theological, metaphysical, and what he called positive as developed in his own teaching; and that this was the first principle of social dynamics. His critics tacitly accepted in principle the possibility of some such division, but they fell to disputing Comte's succession of phases as though this were essential to the law. Comte's idea of applying the rule had nothing to do with the validity of the rule itself. Once it was admitted that human thought had passed through three known phases, — analogous to the chemical phases of solid, liquid, and gaseous, — the standard of measurement which was to be applied might vary with every experimenter until the most convenient should be agreed upon. The commonest objection to Comte's rule, — the objection that the three phases had always existed and still exist, together, — had still less to do with the validity of the law. The residuum of every distillate contains all the original elements in equilibrium with the whole series, if the process is not carried too far. The three phases always exist together in equilibrium; but their limits on either side are fixed by changes of temperature and pressure, manifesting themselves in changes of Direction or Form.

Discarding, then, as unessential, the divisions of history suggested by Comte, the physicist-historian would assume that a change of phase was to be recognized by a change of Form; that is, by a change of Direction; and that it was caused by Acceleration, and increase of Volume or Concentration. In this sense the experimenter is restricted rigidly to the search for changes of Direction or Form of thought, but has no concern in its acceleration except as one of the three variables to which he has to assign mathematical values in order to fix the critical point of change. The first step in experiment is to decide upon some particular and unquestioned change of Direction or Form in human thought.

By common consent, one period of history has always been regarded, even by itself, as a Renaissance, and has boasted of its singular triumph in breaking the continuity of Thought. The exact date of this revolution varies within a margin of two hundred years or more, according as the student fancies the chief factor to have been the introduction of printing, the discovery of America, the invention of the telescope, the writings of Galileo, Descartes, and Bacon, or the mechanical laws perfected by Newton, Huyghens, and the mathematicians as late as 1700; but no one has ever doubted the fact of a distinct change in direction and form of thought during that period; which furnishes the necessary starting-point for any experimental study of historical Phase.

Any one who reads half a dozen pages of Descartes or Bacon sees that these great reformers expressly aimed at changing the Form of thought; that they had no idea but to give it new direction, as Columbus and Galileo had expressly intended to affect direction in space; and even had they all been unconscious of intent, the Church would have pointed it out to them, as it did with so much emphasis to Galileo in 1633.   On this point there was no difference of opinion; the change of direction in Thought was not a mere acceleration; it was an angle or tangent so considerable that the Church in vain tried to ignore it.   Galileo proved it, and the Church agreed with him on that point if on no other.   Nothing could be more unanimously admitted than the change of direction between the thought of St. Augustine and that of Lord Bacon.

Since the Rule of historical Phase has got to rest on this admission, theory cannot venture on the next step unless this one is abundantly proved; but, in fact, no one as yet has ever doubted it.   The moment was altogether the most vital that history ever recorded, and left the deepest impression on men's memory, but this popular impression hardly expresses its scientific value.   As a change of phase it offered singular interest, because, in this case alone, the process could be followed as though it were electrolytic, and the path of each separate molecule were visible under the microscope.   Any school-boy could plot on a sheet of paper in abscissae and ordinates the points through which the curve of thought passed, as fixed by the values of the men and their inventions or discoveries.   History offers no other demonstration to compare with it, and the more because the curve shows plainly that the new lines of Force or Thought were induced lines, obeying the laws of mass, and not those of self-induction.   On this obedience Lord Bacon dwelt with tireless persistence; "the true and legitimate object of science is only to endow human life with new inventions and forces"; but he defined the attractive power of this magnet as equal to the sum of nature's forces, so far as they could serve man's needs or wishes; and he followed that attraction precisely as Columbus followed the attraction of a new world, or as Newton suffered the law of gravitation on his mind as he did on his body.   As each newly appropriated force increased the attraction between the sum of nature's forces and the volume of human mind, by the usual law of squares, the acceleration hurried society towards the critical point that marked the passage into a new phase as though it were heat impelling water to explode as steam.

Only the electrolytic process permits us to watch such movements in physics and chemistry, and the change of phase in 1500–1700 is marvellously electrolytic, but the more curious because we can even give names to the atoms or molecules that passed over to the positive or negative electrode, and can watch the accumulation of force which ended at last by deflecting the whole current

υ

of Thought. The maximum movement possible in the old channel was exceeded; the acceleration and concentration, or volume, reached the point of sudden expansion, and the new phase began.

The history of the new phase has no direct relation with that which preceded it. The gap between theology and mathematics was so sharp in its rapid separation that history is much perplexed to maintain the connection. The earlier signs of the coming change, — before 1500 — were mostly small additions to the commoner mechanical resources of society; but when, after 1500, these additions assumed larger scope and higher aim, they still retained mechanical figure and form even in expanding the law of gravitation into astronomical space. If a direct connection between the two phases is more evident on one line than on another, it is in the curious point of view that society seemed to take of Newton's extension of the law of gravitation to include astronomical mass, which, for two hundred years, resembled an attribute of divinity, and grew into a mechanical theory of the universe amounting to a religion. The connection of thought lay in the human reflection of itself in the universe; yet the acceleration of the seventeenth century, as compared with that of any previous age, was rapid, and that of the eighteenth was startling. The acceleration became even measurable, for it took the form of utilizing heat as force, through the steam-engine, and this addition of power was measurable in the coal output. Society followed the same lines of attraction with little change, down to 1840, when the new chemical energy of electricity began to deflect the thought of society again, and Faraday rivalled Newton in the vigor with which he marked out the path of changed attractions, but the purely mechanical theory of the universe typified by Newton and Dalton held its own, and reached its highest authority towards 1870, or about the time when the dynamo came into use.

Throughout these three hundred years, and especially in the nineteenth century, the acceleration suggests at once the old, familiar law of squares. The curve resembles that of the vaporization of water. The resemblance is too close to be disregarded, for nature loves the logarithm, and perpetually recurs to her inverse square. For convenience, if only as a momentary refuge, the physicist-historian will probably have to try the experiment of taking the law of inverse squares as his standard of social acceleration for the nineteenth century, and consequently for the whole phase, which obliges him to accept it experimentally as a general law of history. Nature is rarely so simple as to act rigorously on the square, but History, like Mathematics, is obliged to assume that eccentricities more or less balance each other, so that something remains constant at last, and it is compelled to approach its problems by means of some fiction,

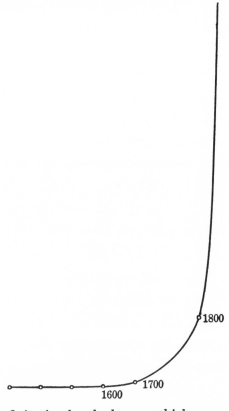

— some infinitesimal calculus, — which may be left as general and undetermined as the formulas of our greatest master, Willard Gibbs, but which gives a hypothetical movement for an ideal substance that can be used for

relation. Some experimental starting-point must always be assumed, and the mathematical historian will be at liberty to assume the most convenient, which is likely to be the rule of geometrical progression.

Thus the first step towards a Rule of Phase for history may be conceived as possible. In fact the Phase may be taken as admitted by all society and every authority since the condemnation of Galileo in 1633; it is only the law, or rule, that the mathematician and physicist would aim at establishing. Supposing, then, that he were to begin by the Phase of 1600–1900, which he might call the Mechanical Phase, and supposing that he assumes for the whole of it the observed acceleration of the nineteenth century, the law of squares, his next step would lead him backward to the far more difficult problem of fixing the limits of the Phase that preceded 1600.

Here was the point which Auguste Comte and all other authorities have failed to agree upon. Although no one denies that at some moment between 1500 and 1700 society passed from one form of thought to another, every one may reasonably hesitate to fix upon the upper limit to be put on the earlier. Comte felt the difficulty so strongly that he subdivided his scale into a fetish, polytheistic, monotheistic, and metaphysical series, before arriving at himself, or Positivism. Most historians would admit the change from polytheism to monotheism, about the year 500, between the establishment of Christianity and that of Mohammedanism as a distinct change in the form or direction of thought, and perhaps in truth society never performed a more remarkable feat than when it consciously unified its religious machinery as it had already concentrated its political and social organism. The concentration certainly marked an era; whether it marked a change of Direction may be disputed. The physicist may prefer to regard it as a refusal to change direction; an obedience to the physico-chemical law that when an equilibrium is subjected to conditions which tend towards change, it reacts internally in ways that tend to resist the external constraint; and, in fact, the establishment of monotheism was regarded by the philosophers even in its own day rather as a reaction than an advance. No doubt the Mohammedan or the Christian felt the change of deity as the essence of religion; but the mathematician might well think that the scope and nature of religion had little to do with the number of Gods. Religion is the recognition of unseen power which has control of man's destiny, and the power which man may, at different times or in different regions, recognize as controlling his destiny, in no way alters his attitude or the form of the thought. The physicist, who affects psychology, will regard religion as the self-projection of mind into nature in one direction, as science is the projection of mind into nature in another.   Both are illusions, as the metaphysician conceives, and in neither case does — or can — the mind reach anything but a different reflection of its own features; but in changing from polytheism to monotheism the mind merely concentrated the image; it was an acceleration, not a direction that was changed.   From first to last the fetish idea inhered in the thought; the idea of an occult power to which obedience was due, — a reflection of the human self from the unknown depths of nature — was as innate in the Allah of Mohammed as in the fetish serpent which Moses made of brass.

The reflection or projection of the mind in nature was the earliest and will no doubt be the last motive of man's mind, whether as religion or as science, and only the attraction will vary according to the value which the mind assigns to the image of the thing that moves it; but the mere concentration of the image need not change the direction of movement, any more than the concentration of converging paths into one single road need change the direction of travel or traffic.   The direction of the social movement may be taken, for scientific purposes, as unchanged from the beginning of history to the condemnation of Galileo which marked the conscious recognition of break in continuity; but in that case the physicist-historian will probably find nowhere the means of drawing any clean line of division across the current of thought, even if he follows it back to the lowest known archaic race.   Notoriously, during this enormously long Religious Phase, the critical point seemed to be touched again and again, — by Greeks and Romans, in Athens, Alexandria, and Constantinople, long before it was finally passed in 1600; but so also, in following the stream backwards to its source, the historian will probably find suggestions of a critical point in ethnology long before such a critical point can be fixed.   So far as he will see, man's thought began by projecting its own image, in this form, into the unknown of nature.   Yet nothing in science is quite so firmly accepted as the fact that such a change of phase took place.   Whether evolution was natural or supernatural, the leap of nature from the phase of instinct to the phase of thought was so immense as to impress itself on every imagination.   No one denies that it must have been relatively ancient; — few anthropologists would be content with less than a hundred thousand years; — and no one need be troubled by admitting that it may have been relatively sudden, like many other mutations, since all the intermediate steps have vanished, and the

line of connection is obliterated.   Yet the anthropoid ape
remains to guide the physical historian, and, what is more
convincing than the ape, the whole phase of instinct survives, not merely as a force in actual evidence, but as the
foundation of the whole geological record.   As an immaterial force, Instinct was so strong as to overcome obstacles that Intellect has been helpless to affect.   The
bird, the beetle, the butterfly accomplished feats that
still defy all the resources of human reason.   The attractions that led instinct to pursue so many and such varied
lines to such great distances, must have been intensely
strong and indefinitely lasting.   The quality that developed the eye and the wing of the bee and the condor has
no known equivalent in man.   The vast perspective of
time opened by the most superficial study of this phase
has always staggered belief ; but geology itself breaks off
abruptly in the middle of the story, when already the
fishes and crustaceans astonish by their modern airs.

Yet the anthropoid ape is assumed to have potentially
contained the future, as he actually epitomized the past ;
and to him, as to us, the phase to which he belonged was
the last and briefest.   Behind him and his so-called
instinct or consciousness, stretched other phases of vegetable and mechanical motion, — more or less organic, —
phases of semi-physical, semi-material, attractions and

repulsions, — that could have, in the concept, no possible limitation of time. Neither bee, nor monkey, nor man, could conceive a time when stones could not fall. The anthropoid ape could look back, as certainly as the most scientific modern historian, to a critical point at which his own phase must have begun, when the rudimentary forces that had developed in the vegetables had acquired a volume and complexity which could no longer be enclosed in rigid forms, and had expanded into freer movement. The ape might have predicted his own expansion into new force, for, long before the first man was sketched, the monkeys and their companions in instinct had peopled every continent, and civilized — according to their standards — the whole world.

The problem to the anthropoid ape a hundred thousand years ago was the same as that addressed to the physicist-historian of 1900 : — How long could he go on developing indefinite new phases in response to the occult attractions of an infinitely extended universe? What new direction could his genius take? To him, the past was a miraculous development, and, to perfect himself, he needed only to swim like a fish and soar like a bird; but probably he felt no conscious need of mind. His phase had lasted unbroken for millions of years, and had produced an absolutely miraculous triumph of instinct. Had he been so far gifted as to foresee his next mutation, he would have possibly found in it only a few meagre pages, telling of impoverished life, at the end of his own enormous library of records, the bulk of which had been lost. Had he studied these past records, he would probably have admitted that thus far, by some mechanism totally incomprehensible, the series of animated beings had in some directions responded to nature's call, and had thrown out tentacles on many sides; but he, as a creature of instinct, would have instinctively wished to develop in the old directions, — he could have felt no conscious wish to become a mathematician.

Thus the physicist-historian seems likely to be forced into admitting that an attractive force, like gravitation, drew these trickling rivulets of energy into new phases by an external influence which tended to concentrate and accelerate their motion by a law with which their supposed wishes or appetites had no conscious relation. At a certain point the electric corpuscle was obliged to become a gas, the gas a liquid, the liquid a solid. For material mass, only one law was known to hold good. Ice, water, and gas, all have weight; they obey the law of astronomical mass; they are guided by the attraction of matter. If the current of Thought has shown obedience to the law of gravitation it is material, and its phases should be easily calculated.

The physicist will, therefore, have to begin by trying the figure of the old Newtonian or Cartesian vortices, or gravitating group of heterogeneous substances moving in space as though in a closed receptacle. Any nebula or vortex-group would answer his purpose, — say the great nebula of Orion, which he would conceive as containing potentially every possible phase of substance. Here the various local centres of attraction would tend to arrange the diffused elements like iron-filings round a magnet in a phase of motion which, if the entire equilibrium were perfect, would last forever; but if, at any point, the equilibrium were disturbed, the whole volume would be set in new motion, until, under the rise in pressure and temperature, one phase after another must mechanically, — and more and more suddenly, — occur with the increasing velocity of movement.

That such sudden changes of phase do in fact occur is one of the articles of astronomical faith, but the reality of the fact has little to do with the convenience of the figure. The nebula is beyond human measurements. A simple figure is needed, and our solar system offers none. The nearest analogy would be that of a comet, not so much because it betrays marked phases, as because it resembles Thought in certain respects, since, in the first place, no one knows what it is, which is also true of

Thought, and it seems in some cases to be immaterial, passing in a few hours from the cold of space to actual contact with the sun at a temperature some two thousand times that of incandescent iron, and so back to the cold of space, without apparent harm, while its tail sweeps round an inconceivable circle with almost the speed of thought, — certainly the speed of light, — and its body may show no nucleus at all. If not a Thought, the comet is a sort of brother of Thought, an early condensation of the ether itself, as the human mind may be another, traversing the infinite without origin or end, and attracted by a sudden object of curiosity that lies by chance near its path. If such elements are subject to the so-called law of gravitation, no good reason can exist for denying gravitation to the mind.

Such a typical comet is that of 1668, or 1843, or Newton's comet of 1680; bodies which fall in a direct line, — itself a miracle, — from space, for some hundreds of years, with an acceleration given by the simple formula $k\,\dfrac{M}{r^2}$, where k is the constant of gravitation, M the mass of the sun and r the distance between the comet and the centre of the sun. If not deflected from its straight course by any of the planets, it penetrates at last within the orbit of Venus, and approaches the sun.

At five o'clock one winter morning in 1843, the comet began to show deflection at about two-and-a-half diameters distance from the sun; at ten o'clock it was abreast of the sun, and swung about at a right angle; at half past ten it passed perihelion at a speed of about 350 miles a second; and at noon, after having passed three hours in a temperature exceeding 5000° Centigrade, it appeared unharmed on its return course, until at five o'clock in the afternoon it was flying back to the space it came from, on the same straight line, parallel to that by which it came.

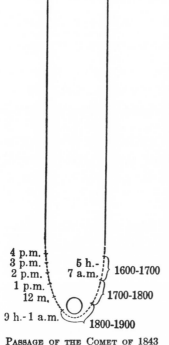

PASSAGE OF THE COMET OF 1843
February 27, twelve hours

Nothing in the behavior of Thought is more paradoxical than that of these planets, or shows direction or purpose more flagrantly, and it happens that they furnish the only astronomical parallel for the calculated acceleration of the last Phase of Thought. No other heavenly body shows the same sharp curve or excessive speed.

Yet, if the calculated curve of deflection of Thought in 1600–1900 were put on that of the planet, it would show that man's evolution had passed perihelion, and that his movement was already retrograde. To some minds, this objection might not seem fatal, and in fact another fifty years must elapse before the rate of human movement would sensibly relax; but another objection would be serious, if not for the theory, at least for the figure. The acceleration of the comet is much slower than that of society. The world did not double or treble its movement between 1800 and 1900, but, measured by any standard known to science — by horse-power, calories, volts, mass in any shape, — the tension and vibration and volume and so-called progression of society were fully a thousand times greater in 1900 than in 1800; — the force had doubled ten times over, and the speed, when measured by electrical standards as in telegraphy, approached infinity, and had annihilated both space and time. No law of material movement applied to it.

Some such result was to be expected. Nature is not so simple as to obey only one law, or to apply necessarily a law of material mass to immaterial substance. The result proves only that the comet is material, and that thought is less material than the comet. The figure serves the physicist only to introduce the problem. If the laws of material mass do not help him, he will seek for a law of immaterial mass, and here he has, as yet, but one analogy to follow, — that of electricity. If the comet, or the current of water, offers some suggestion for the current of human society, electricity offers one so much stronger that psychologists are apt instinctively to study the mind as a phase of electro-magnetism. Whether such a view is sound, or not, matters nothing to its convenience as a figure. Thought has always moved under the incumbrance of matter, like an electron in a solution, and, unless the conditions are extremely favorable, it does not move at all, as has happened in many solutions, — as in China, — or in some cases may become enfeebled and die out, without succession. Only by watching its motion on the enormous scale of historical and geological or biological time can one see, — across great gulfs of ignorance, — that the current has been constant as measured by its force and volume in the absorption of nature's resources, and that, within the last century, its acceleration has been far more rapid than before, — more rapid than can be accounted for by the laws of material mass; but only highly trained physicists could invent a model to represent such motion. The ignorant student can merely guess what the skilled experimenter would do; he can only imagine an ideal case.

This ideal case would offer to his imagination the figure of nature's power as an infinitely powerful dynamo, attracting or inducing a current of human thought according to the usual electric law of squares, — that is to say, that the average motion of one phase is the square of that which precedes it. The curve is thus : —

Assuming that the change of phase began in 1500, and that the new Mechanical Phase dates in its finished form from Galileo, Bacon, and Descartes, with a certain lag in its announcement by them, — say from 1600, — the law of squares gives a curve like that of ice, water, and steam, running off to the infinite in almost straight lines at either end, like the comet, but at right angles. Supposing a value in numbers of any sort, — say 6, 36, 1296, — and assigning 1296 to the period 1600–1900, the preceding religious phase would have a value of only 36 as the average of many thousand years, representing therefore nearly a straight line, while the twentieth century would be represented by the square of 1296 or what is equivalent to a straight line to infinity.

Reversing the curve to try the time-sequence by the same rule, the Mechanical Phase being represented by 300 years, the Religious Phase would require not less than 90,000. Perhaps this result might not exactly suit a physicist's views, but if he accepts the sequence

x

90,000 and 300 for these two phases in time, he arrives at some curious results for the future, and in calculating the period of the fourth, or electric phase, he must be prepared for extreme figures.

No question in the series is so vital as that of fixing the limits of the Mechanical Phase. Assuming, as has been done, the year 1600 for its beginning, the question remains to decide the probable date of its close. Perhaps the physicist might regard it as already closed. He might say that the highest authority of the mechanical universe was reached about 1870, and that, just then, the invention of the dynamo turned society sharply into a new channel of electric thought as different from the mechanical as electric mass is different from astronomical mass. He might assert that Faraday, Clerk Maxwell, Hertz, Helmholz, and the whole electro-magnetic school, thought in terms quite unintelligible to the old chemists and mechanists. The average man, in 1850, could understand what Davy or Darwin had to say; he could not understand what Clerk Maxwell meant. The later terms were not translatable into the earlier; even the mathematics became hyper-mathematical. Possibly a physicist might go so far as to hold that the most arduous intellectual effort ever made by man with a distinct consciousness of needing new mental powers, was made after 1870 in the general effort to acquire habits of electro-magnetic thought, — the familiar use of formulas carrying indefinite self-contradiction into the conception of force. The physicist knows best his own difficulties, and perhaps to him the process of evolution may seem easy, but to the mere by-stander the gap between electric and astronomic mass seems greater than that between Descartes and St. Augustine, or Lord Bacon and Thomas Aquinas. The older ideas, though hostile, were intelligible; the idea of electro-magnetic-ether is not.

Thus it seems possible that another generation, trained after 1900 in the ideas and terms of electro-magnetism and radiant matter, may regard that date as marking the sharpest change of direction, taken at the highest rate of speed, ever effected by the human mind; a change from the material to the immaterial, — from the law of gravitation to the law of squares. The Phases were real: the change of direction was measured by the consternation of physicists and chemists at the discovery of radium which was quite as notorious as the consternation of the Church at the discovery of Galileo; but it is the affair of science, not of historians, to give it a mathematical value.

Should the physicist reject the division, and insist on the experience of another fifty or a hundred years, the consequence would still be trifling for the fourth term of the series. Supposing the Mechanical Phase to have lasted 300 years, from 1600 to 1900, the next or Electric Phase would have a life equal to $\sqrt{300}$, or about seventeen years and a half, when — that is, in 1917 — it would pass into another or Ethereal Phase, which, for half a century, science has been promising, and which would last only $\sqrt{17.5}$, or about four years, and bring Thought to the limit of its possibilities in the year 1921.   It may well be!   Nothing whatever is beyond the range of possibility; but even if the life of the previous phase, 1600–1900, were extended another hundred years, the difference to the last term of the series would be negligible.   In that case, the Ethereal Phase would last till about 2025.

The mere fact that society should think in terms of Ether or the higher mathematics might mean little or much.   According to the Phase Rule, it lived from remote ages in terms of fetish force, and passed from that into terms of mechanical force, which again led to terms of electric force, without fairly realizing what had happened except in slow social and political revolutions. Thought in terms of Ether means only Thought in terms of itself, or, in other words, pure Mathematics and Metaphysics, a stage often reached by individuals.   At the utmost it could mean only the subsidence of the current into an ocean of potential thought, or mere consciousness, which is also possible, like static electricity. The only consequence might be an indefinitely long stationary period, such as John Stuart Mill foresaw. In that case, the current would merely cease to flow.

But if, in the prodigiously rapid vibration of its last phases, Thought should continue to act as the universal solvent which it is, and should reduce the forces of the molecule, the atom, and the electron to that costless servitude to which it has reduced the old elements of earth and air, fire and water; if man should continue to set free the infinite forces of nature, and attain the control of cosmic forces on a cosmic scale, the consequences may be as surprising as the change of water to vapor, of the worm to the butterfly, of radium to electrons. At a given volume and velocity, the forces that are concentrated on his head must act.

Such seem to be, more or less probably, the lines on which any physical theory of the universe would affect the study of history, according to the latest direction of physics. Comte's Phases adapt themselves easily to some such treatment, and nothing in philosophy or metaphysics forbids it. The figure used for illustration is immaterial except so far as it limits the nature of the attractive force. In any case the theory will have to assume that the mind has always figured its motives as reflections of itself, and that this is as true in its conception of electricity as in its instinctive imitation of a God. Always and everywhere the mind creates its own universe, and pursues its own phantoms; but the force behind the image is always a reality, — the attractions of occult power. If values can be given to these attractions, a physical theory of history is a mere matter of physical formula, no more complicated than the formulas of Willard Gibbs or Clerk Maxwell; but the task of framing the formula and assigning the values belongs to the physicist, not to the historian; and if one such arrangement fails to accord with the facts, it is for him to try another, to assign new values to his variables, and to verify the results. The variables themselves can hardly suffer much change.

If the physicist-historian is satisfied with neither of the known laws of mass, — astronomical or electric, — and cannot arrange his variables in any combination that will conform with a phase-sequence, no resource seems to remain but that of waiting until his physical problems shall be solved, and he shall be able to explain what Force is. As yet he knows almost as little of material as of immaterial substance. He is as perplexed before the phenomena of Heat, Light, Magnetism, Electricity, Gravitation, Attraction, Repulsion, Pressure, and the whole schedule of names used to indicate unknown elements, as before the common, infinitely familiar fluctuations of his own Thought whose action is so astounding on the direction of his energies.   Probably the solution of any one of the problems will give the solution for them all.

WASHINGTON, January 1, 1909.

INDEX

Acceleration, movement of, 289.

Adams, Brooks, inheritance, vii; introduction, xi; relations with Henry Adams, 1, 88; "Emancipation of Massachusetts," 87; "Law of Civilization and Decay," 88; a forecast, 116.

Adams, Charles Francis, 75.

Adams, Charles Francis, Jr., 88.

Adams family, 93.

Adams, Henry, scientific methods, viii; pose in "Education," 6, 103; "Theory of Phase," 7; aptitude for science, 35; "Law of Civilization and Decay," 90, 99; letter to Am. Historical Assn., 96, 125; on arrested civilization, 98; on democracy's failure, 108; prediction of catastrophe, 111, 115; "Letter to Teachers of History," 112, 137; "Theory of Phase in History," 113; belief in chaos, 122; "Tendency of History," 125.

Adams, John, 42, 93; on report on weights, 46.

Adams, John Quincy, 113; faith in democracy, v, 77; faith in God, vi, 26, 28, 33, 53, 76; a scientist, 9, 52; tragedy of presidency, 10; internal improvements, 20, 25, 107; resolution, 21n; resigns from Senate, 21; Missouri question, 23; slavery, 23, 29; letter to Upham, 24; scientific development of internal resources, 29; letter to J. Edwards, 29; reflections on belief, 33; ambitions, 34; report on weights and measures, ix, 37; live-oak forest, 52; elected to Congress, 55; Smithson bequest, 58; on astronomy, 59; invited to Cincinnati, 63; journey, 68; results of his influence, 73; on Jackson, 77; civil service, 81; duration of Union, 107; belief in chaos, 122.

Adams, Louisa Catherine, 75.

Adams, Thomas Boylston, 47.

Agassiz, Louis, on man, 177.

Ancients, battle with moderns, 245.

Animals, stunting of, 227.

Anthropologists, on evolution, 170.

Ape, anthropoid, 297.

Archiac, Étienne Jules Adolphe Desmier de Saint Simon, Vicomte d', 162.

Arndt, Friedrich, 176, 237.

Association, American Historical, H. Adams' letter as president, 125.

Astronomy, J. Q. Adams on, 60; favored by government, 73; science of chaos, 122.

Attraction, 280.

Bache, Alexander Dallas, petition for observatories, 58.

Bacon, Francis, 287; object of science, 289.

Bancroft, George, 147.

Bankers, influence of, 120.

Benton, Thomas Hart, 32, 33.

Bergson, Henri, life as forces, 204.

Bernouilli, ——, 190.

Bigelow, Jacob, 75.

Blandet, ——, 162, 164, 166.

Branch, John, 53.

Branca, Wilhelm, 176, 237.

Brooks, Peter Chardon, 63.

Brunhes, Bernhard, philosophy of history, 254, 258.

Buckle, Henry Thomas, 126.

Bumstead, Henry Andrews, consulted on scientific question, ix.

Calhoun, John Caldwell, 44.

Canals, projected by Washington, 14; travelling by, 68.

Canning, Stratford, 41, 44.

Capital of nation, Washington's conception, 17.

Carnot, Nicolas Léonhard Sadi, 141.

313

Catastrophe, law of energy, 148.
Centre, economic, of world, 109.
Chaos of democratic mediocrity, 115; astronomy, science of, 122.
Child, creature of state, 260.
Church and a science of history, 129, 131.
Ciamician, Giacomo, 196; vital energy and will, 193.
Cincinnati, observatory, 63.
Clausius, Rudolf Julius Emmanuel, 140, 231.
Clay, Henry, internal improvements, 21; on civil service, 82; on the future, 83.
Comet, 300; of 1843, 302.
Communism, 130, 131.
Competition, 78, 79, 85; war and, 116.
Comte, Auguste, 284, 309; phases of the human mind, 285, 293.
Consciousness defined, 204.
Cope, Edward Drinker, on descent of man, 172.
Corwin, Thomas, 70.
Cotton, invention of gin, 22, 31.
Currency, effect of debasement, 95.

Dalton, John, 190.
Dana, James Dwight, on stunting animal life, 227.
Darwin, Charles, 218; influence of, 126, 128; optimism, 130; law of evolution, 152, 159, 196; evolution of man, 170; on the eye, 226; energy in theory, 241.
Dastre, Jules Albert Frank, on vital energy, 154.
Davies, Charles, on report on weights, 49.
Davis, Charles Henry, 57.
Decrepitude, social, signs of, 186.
Dedham, Mass., meeting, 67.
Degradation of energy, 83, 108; beginning of, 167; universities and, 245; final word, 256.
Degradationist, position of, 157.
Democracy, degradation, 84, 104, 108, 121; failure, 84.
Descartes, René, 262, 287; on man, 232.
Direction, in science, 279, 286.
Dissipation of energy, law of, 141, 152, 154, 179.

Dollo, Louis, law of evolution, 170.
Driesch, Hans, "Vitalismus," 147; on descent, 250.
Drosera, 242.
Durkheim, Emile, pessimism, 188.

Earth, shrinkage of the, 165.
Education, of waste or conservation, 78; and hesitation, 186.
Edwards, Justin, letter of J. Q. Adams, 29, 80.
Electricity, 274, 304.
"Emancipation of Massachusetts," 88.
Energy, degradation of, 83, 195; law of conservation, 140, 154, 209; law of dissipation, 141, 152, 154, 179, 212; solar, 143, 148, 164; vital, 146, 149, 154, 193, 201, 221; social, 154; reason, 192; will, 193; thought, 207; economy of, 215; development of physical, 233.
Entropy, law of, 142, 154, 209, 242, 251.
Equilibrium, stable, 248, 258; defined, 267.
Ether, 275, 308; universal solvent, 270; a phase, 278.
Evolution, 210, 231; Darwin on, 152; change in discussion, 170; Dollo's law, 170; upward, 244.
Evolutionist, conquests of, 157; dilemma of, 214; compromise, 256.
Experience, limit of, 272.
Eye, complexity, 226.

Family, dissolution of modern, 2, 119; origin and woman's share, 3.
Faraday, Michael, 272, 273, 291.
Faye, Hervé Auguste Étienne Albans, on end of universe, 149.
Flammarion, Camille, 184, 189; solar catastrophe, 182.
Flechsig, Paul, brain and will, 200.
Flemming, *Sir* Sandford, on report on weights, 50.
Fluid, 274.
Ford, Worthington Chauncey, x.
Form, 286.
Franklin, Benjamin, 285.
Free-will, 232.

Galileo Galilei, 132, 220, 287.
Gallatin, Albert, report on internal improvements, 21.

Gary, Elbert Henry, 116.
Gaudry, Jean Albert, 167, 226, 227.
Geologists, teaching, 166; on ice-cap, 179.
Ghent, peace commissioners, 118.
Gibbon, Edward 245.
Gibbs, Josiah Willard, 190; rule of phases, 237, 267.
Gilliss, James Melville, 57.
Gold-bugs, 96.
Goldscheid, Rudolph, on direction, 279.
Grasset, weakness of will, 253.
Gray, Andrew, on death of all things, 150.
Great Britain and the United States, 114.
Grinnell, Joseph, 70.
Guy de Lusignan, faith in the cross, 54.

Haeckel, Ernst Heinrich, evolution, 153, 156; of man, 171.
Hallock, William, on report on weights, 51.
Hartmann, Eduard von, 193, 196, 204, 231; end of vital processes, 151.
Harvard University, degree for Jackson, 77.
Heat, Voss on, 270.
Heer, Oswald, 166; arctic flora, 160.
Helmholtz, Hermann Ludwig Ferdinand von, 140, 231.
Hertz, Heinrich Rudolf, 277.
History, tendency of, 126; science of, 126, 148; teaching of, 97, 189, 210, 261; science of vital energy, 207; and degradation, 243; Brunhes on, 255; rule of phase, 267; matter and processes, 280; and physics, 283; mechanical phase, 293, 305; electrical phase, 308.
Hopf, Ludwig, 174, 175, 176, 237.
Huxley, Thomas Henry, 178.
Hyper-thought, 276.

Inertia, 158.
Intellect and instinct, 206.

Jackson, Andrew, internal improvements, 21, 27; in Florida, 22; principle of evil and a barbarian, 77; abuse of office, 82.
Jefferson, Thomas, on slavery, 18.
Johnson, William Cost, 70.

Joly, John, 239.
Jones, Mrs. Mary C., advises on introduction, xii.

Kelvin, Lord, see William Thomson.
Kendall, Amos, 53.
Kerner, Anton, on vital force, 147.
Klaatsch, Hermann, on human teeth, 174; primitive man, 240.
Krainsky, N. 197.

Labor, and a science of history, 129.
Lalande, André, on thought, 203.
Lands, public, a national trust, 27; dissipated, 31.
Lapparent, Albert Auguste Cochon de, diminution of solar heat, 163, 164; vegetation, 167, 168; on future of earth, 168, 184.
Law of dissipation of energy, 141.
Law, origin of municipal, 80; weakness of human codes, 80.
"Law of Civilization and Decay," 88, 99.
Le Bon, Gustave, 254; on the crowd, 252; enfeeblement of will, 253.
Lemur, hypothetical, 172.
Lex Poppaea, 187.
Light-houses of the sky, 61.
Littré, Émile, 285.
Live-oak, J. Q. Adams' interest, 52.
Loeb, Jacques, 197; will and mechanical action, 198.
London, financial supremacy, 110.
Lunacy, increase of, 254.
Lyell, Sir Charles, H. Adams and, 35; law of uniformity, 153, 159, 165.

Macaulay, Thomas Babington, Lord, 147, 186, 245.
McLean, John, and public office, 82.
Man, an automaton, vii; appearance of, 161, 167; limit of development, 170; evolution, 171; end of series, 177; and nature, 214, 229; wastefulness of, 216; no creative energy, 230; primitive, 240; mental development, 259.
Mason, George, on slavery, 18.
Massachusetts, Emancipation of, 88.
Mathematics in physics, 272.
Maury, Matthew Fontaine, 57.
Maxwell, James Clerk, 279.

Maysville road veto, 28.
Metaphysics and physics, 196.
Meyer, Eduard, man's mental development, 259.
Mill, John Stuart, 285, 309.
Missouri question, J. Q. Adams on, 23.
Mitchel, Ormsby McKnight, Cincinnati observatory, 63.
Mitchell, Thomas R., 21.
Moderns, battle with ancients, 245.
Monism, 240.
"Mont St. Michel and Chartres," 2, 102.
Morgan, Jacques Jean Marie de, 184; on future of earth, 181.
Motion, potential, in space, 270.

Nebula of Orion, 300.
Newcomb, Simon, 122.
Newton, *Sir* Isaac, 290.
Nietzsche, Friedrich Wilhelm, 196.
Nourse, Joseph Everett, 59.

Observatory, naval, 58; Adams' name for, 61; Cincinnati, 63.
Office, theory of public, 81.
Orion, nebula of, 300.
Ostwald, Wilhelm, 197, 236; on Kelvin's law, 142, 154; motion of mind, 198.

Panmixia, 235.
Paris, peace commissioners at, 117.
Pasley, *Sir* Charles William, on report on weights, 48.
Peirce, Benjamin, 5.
Pendulum measurements, 41.
Perfectability, human, 30, 53; Darwin on, 130, 159.
Pessimism, 257.
Phase, in History, Theory of, 114; rule of, 237, 267; defined, 267; hierarchy of, 274.
Physicist, explanation of history, 213; use of energies, 243.
Physics and metaphysics, 197.
Poincaré, Jules Henri, on monism, 240.
Poincaré, Lucien, 242; anarchy in science, 239.
Pressure, 280.
Property, and a science of history, 129.
Psychologists, on energy, 197.
Psychology, physical, 234.

Radium, 277, **307.**
Reason and tropism, 198; **energy and,** 208, 229; accounting for, 242.
Reformation, the, 111.
Reinke, Johannes, 204, 239; on *energetik,* 258.
Relics, fall into disfavor, 54.
Religion, 294.
Renaissance, **287.**
Rome, fall of, 89.
Rosa, extinction of species, 170, 177.
Rosenstiehl, A., 270.
Rousseau, Jean Jacques, 128, 237; on the thinker, 203.
Rush, Richard, 58; on report on weights, 45.
Rutledge, John, on slavery, 19.

St. Paul, on competition of flesh and spirit, 85, 105.
Saporta, Louis Charles Joseph Gaston, Marquis de, 225; vegetation, 160, 167.
Schopenhauer, Arthur, 196; will as energy, 193.
Science of history, 127; absolute, 129; chaos of, 239.
Scudder, Horace Elisha, 87.
Slavery, Washington's views, 18; Virginian opposition, 18; compromise in constitution, 19; suppression of trade, 22, 28; extinction of, 29.
Smith, Adam, 128.
Smithson, James, bequest, 58.
Socialism, 130.
Society, decadence of, 247; an organism, 258.
Sociologists, on society, 186, 188.
Solids, 274.
Solution, definition of, 269.
Space, 275.
State, and a science of history, 129.
Stewart, Balfour, 232.
Stoney, G. Johnstone, 274.
Sun, condensation of, 164; economy of, 218.
Swift, Jonathan, "Battle of the Books," 245.

Tait, Peter Guthrie, 145.
Teeth, human, number of, 174.
Temperature, 280.

Tendency of history, 125.

Thayer, Minot, 67.

Thomson, Hanna, on brain and will, 199.

Thomson, William, Lord Kelvin, 140, 220, 231; dissipation of energy, 145, 152, 162; on will, 201; exhaustion of oxygen, 216; confession of failure, 238.

Thought, nature of, 203, 273; as motion, 219; solvent of, 281; and phase, 283; deflection curve, 303; acceleration, 303.

Time, change of value, 222.

Topinard, Paul, on human brain, 175, 176; end of earth, 177; man and nature, 178.

Trade union, principle of the, 121.

Transformation, 191, 210, 241.

Turgot, Anne Robert Jacques, 285.

Tyndall, John, on solar energy, 143.

Uniformity, law of, Lyell's, 153, 159, 165.

United States, civil war, object of, vii; and Great Britain, 114.

Unity, 241.

Universities, Washington's, 17, 106; evolution upward, 244; degradation dogma, 245.

Upham, Charles Wentworth, letter of J. Q. Adams, 24.

Vapor, 274.

Vegetation, changes in, 160; climax, 167.

Vibration, and direction, 279.

Vienna, Congress of, 118.

Virginia and slavery, 18, 22; and industry, 106.

Vitalists, 146.

Volume, 281.

Voss, Isaac, defintion of heat, 270.

Vulpian, Edme Félix Alfred, human brain, 175.

Wade, Herbert T., on report on weights, 51.

Wagner, Richard, 246.

War, breeders of, 80, 116.

Washington, George, constructive theory, 14, 106; capital city, 17; university, 17, 106; slavery, 18; personality, 84, 104; idea of government, 105; body of, 107.

Washington, John Augustine, 107.

Washington city, poverty in scientific appliances, 42.

Weights and measures, J. Q. Adams' report, 37; metric system, 39.

Whitney, Eli, cotton gin, 22, 31.

Will as energy, 193, 199, 208; brain and, 200; enfeeblement of, 253.

Winslow, Forbes, on degeneration, 254.

Woman and the family, 3; degradation of, 111; unsexing of, 118.

Wundt, Wilhelm Max, 197.

Wyeth, George, on slavery, 18.

Zittel, Karl Alfred von, on descent, 250.

Printed in the United States of America.

This special edition of

THE DEGRADATION OF THE
DEMOCRATIC DOGMA

by Henry Adams

has been privately printed for the members of
The Classics of Liberty Library by Quebecor
Printing Kingsport. Film was prepared from the
first edition of 1919. New type matter was com-
posed by P&M Typesetting, Inc., in Century.
The text paper was especially made for this
edition by the P. H. Glatfelter Company. The
volume has been quarter-bound in genuine
leather by Quebecor Printing Sherwood. End-
leaves are a specially commissioned design of
Richard J. Wolfe. Edges are gilded; the spine is
stamped in 22-karat gold. Cover stampings and
design of the edition are by Daniel B. Bianchi
and Selma Ordewer.

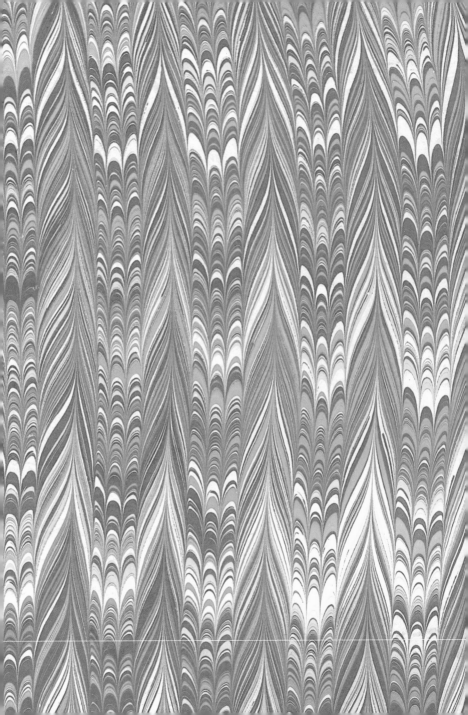